Healthcare Business Intelligence

Healthcare Business Intelligence

A Guide to Empowering Successful Data Reporting and Analytics

LAURA B. MADSEN, MS

WILEY

John Wiley & Sons, Inc.

Library of Congress Cataloging-in-Publication Data:

Madsen, Laura B., 1973–
   Healthcare business intelligence : a guide to empowering successful
data reporting and analytics / Laura B. Madsen.
     p. cm.
   Includes index.
   ISBN 978-1-118-21780-1 (hardback);   ISBN 978-1-118-28233-5 (ebk);
   ISBN 978-1-118-28394-3 (ebk);   ISBN 978-1-118-28490-2 (ebk)
   1. Medical records–Management.   2. Business intelligence.   I. Title.
RA976.M24 2012
651.5′04261–dc23   2012012398

Printed in the United States of America

10 9 8 7 6 5 4 3 2 1

To Karl and Nolan

Contents

Contents

Foreword

A year ago, senior managers at my hospital asked me a simple question in anticipation of healthcare reform:

Can you create the omnibus platform for coordination, population health, and care management that integrates heterogeneous data from large and small affiliated provider organizations, supplying retrospective and prospective analytics to improve quality, safety and efficiency?

No problem.

Everyone wants to be an accountable care organization, but no one knows how to do it.

I believe there are five tactics necessary for success in a world where reimbursement for quality rather than quantity is our future:

1. Universal adoption of electronic health records
2. Healthcare information exchange
3. Business intelligence/analytics
4. Universal availability of personal health records to patients/families
5. Decision support at the point of care

This book is about how to achieve number 3.

Analyzing data requires much more than technology—it requires an understanding of the very nature of the data and its intended uses. What do I mean?

A few years ago I hired an analyst who looked at one of our data marts and concluded that the average length of stay in the operating room was 127 days! They did not know that length of stay in hospitals is measured in days but in operating rooms it is in minutes.

Another analyst noted that no inpatients over the age of 65 had ever visited our emergency department. They did not realize that Medicare creates a bundled payment for all care delivered in an encounter—there is no separate emergency department charge.

This book provides all the tools necessary to implement successful analytics from an understanding of data quality to getting the project done via appropriate governance. Tactics discussed include the right scope of analytics projects to maximize value while reducing costs and time to deliver useful results. Managing data security, ensuring data integrity, and managing the impact of analytics on culture are key topics that I'm focused on every day. This book shares the details from trenches.

I know you'll find this book to be a helpful reference for your business intelligence journey. It nicely summarizes all the lessons I've learned over the past decade, so you'll have the benefit of best practices without having to repeat our mistakes!

Dr. John Halamka

Preface

Twenty years ago, I sat in a doctor's office and received a diagnosis that would change my life forever. Although I was fortunate that my diagnosis was chronic but not life-threatening, it took years of suffering before someone could tell me what was wrong. Each doctor I went to see requested the same information, the same replay of history and symptoms, and after three years of begging for relief the paper copy of my medical record came to rival Webster's unabridged dictionary. I didn't know or understand then that most of the inefficiencies within the healthcare system had nothing to do with the capabilities of the care team—and everything to do with sharing data.

Fast-forward to 2006, when my nearly two-year-old nephew sat in the emergency room of Children's Hospital in Minneapolis. He had been sick on and off for about a month, not terribly unusual for a two-year-old, but his regular doctor was concerned enough to send him and his parents to Children's. It was the Tuesday afternoon before Thanksgiving. I had just walked in the door at home when my sister called me and told me that a blood test revealed that my nephew had leukemia. In less than 36 hours, on a holiday week, he received his first treatment. We sat Thanksgiving morning in the waiting room staring at a TV screen that looked more like a report. It had the patient name, location (e.g., prep, recovery) with a green/red symbol to help identify whether he was passing between them. I was struck with the level, ease, and sophistication of the data that Children's Hospital uses every day to keep their patients and families healthy and well informed. Today, my nephew is a thriving seven-year-old.

There's no doubt that healthcare is deeply personal. The work that I do assists providers in taking better care of people like me and you. Sometimes that means a direct impact to patient care, and sometimes it means that it makes it easier for them to run the business side of providing care. But every day I recognize that the value that data provides means more efficiency, better outcomes, and improved transparency. And we all benefit in the end.

Today, as the arguments for and against universal healthcare continue, we all recognize that the fundamental structure of the U.S. healthcare system is broken. I don't claim that better use and management of data is the panacea, but I do strongly believe that it's as close to a magic bullet as anything else we have in our arsenal.

There is no better time, as data volumes increase due to regulatory pressures, to take advantage of all we have learned to create strong data management programs in every healthcare organization. The result of this will be a stronger and better health information exchange; a better understanding of members, patients, and behaviors; payment transparency; easier transitions between providers (inpatient to outpatient, or just moving geographically); improved data on drug-drug interactions; the list goes on and on.

In the information technology (IT) industry terminology the term for this type of data management work is *business intelligence* (BI).

This book was born out of my work in healthcare business intelligence, more specifically, my work in creating healthcare BI programs. Almost every organization I have worked with has asked the same questions and expressed similar concerns. Business intelligence is a top-10 trend for just about every chief information officer (CIO) in the country. Healthcare as an industry is behind in adopting BI, yet no other industry needs it more. The demand for data management expertise in healthcare is increasing at a rapid rate, but the resource pool is limited, especially if you are looking for someone who has built BI programs specifically for healthcare. The lack of industry knowledge and experience jeopardizes healthcare organizations' chances of success in implementing and adopting BI. As a result, many programs fail at things that they shouldn't fail at, or focus on things that are not important.

This book was written with the business leader in mind. You will not find in these pages a detailed method for building out data models (that book has been written well by others). What you will find is a guidebook for creating a BI program that will become a sustaining capability and will provide your organization with significant value. This book differs from the others written about BI. First, it focuses on healthcare, and second, it focuses on the business leader interested in BI.

The following chapters are what I consider the tenets of successful healthcare BI programs. A healthcare BI program can exist without some or all of these, but it may be on shaky ground. The challenges with healthcare BI programs are significant, from the technical to the process. The statistics continue to be disturbing: more than 70 percent of BI programs fail on their first attempt. Many factors are associated with failure for BI programs, but these tenets have been built based on my years of experience in building healthcare BI programs. I know what happens to healthcare BI programs without these tenets; they're on a fast track to disappointment.

So, how can you avoid becoming just another statistic? Use this book as your guide, your cookbook if you will, for creating your program. Why a cookbook? I have been cooking since I could reach a countertop (that's a completely different book) and what I have learned in cooking is that two cooks can follow the same recipe and have the dish turn out quite differently. That's okay, as long as they have all the right ingredients and a step-by-step process for completion. The same must be true for a healthcare BI program. Your conditions will vary. Your hospital or health plan is not just like any other organization; in order for your healthcare BI program to succeed it must (repeat, *must*) be created, molded, and formed to your organization. The things that work for one hospital may not work for the hospital across the street. That's okay, as long as we all have the same ingredients.

This book gives you the ingredients and, where appropriate, step-by-step process for including key factors. In addition, you will see throughout the book key points highlighted, mini case studies that are meant to provide you with an understanding of what healthcare organizations can achieve when they manage their data as an asset, and sections on how to put all the pieces together.

After reading this book, you will be able to:

- Articulate the best practices of business intelligence and data warehouses for healthcare
- Assess your organization's preparedness to adopt BI
- Create a shared corporate lexicon
- Operationalize a BI program
- Build supporting processes and infrastructures to support a BI program today and in the future
- Present the value proposition and return on investment (ROI) to executives
- Proactively market the BI program to stakeholders

Acknowledgments

It is December 2011 and I am about halfway through the content for this book. I am pausing here, at this time and place, to remind myself why I am doing this. I have found it easy in this process to get wrapped up in the length of the chapters or the tone of a sentence. I have found that the more lost I get in these details the less I remember what drives me.

My intention for this book is relatively simple: to start a conversation, to ask why the industry is what it is (or isn't). I do this because of the laser-like focus and incredibly idealist proposition that starting this conversation, pushing the envelope, can drive changes in healthcare. Although I am an idealist, I am also a realistic, so I recognize that this one book about data and reporting will likely not change healthcare in any measureable way. People much smarter than me have been trying to fix the situation for years and haven't been successful, but I am proud to be part of the group that has tried.

In August 2008 I sat down with Tom Niccum, president of Lancet. We had discussed the possibility of my joining Lancet. During this conversation we first discussed the idea of a book. In 2008 the idea of a healthcare BI book was questionable. Healthcare had not adopted BI, and although the elections were looming, none of us knew the degree to which the administration would impact healthcare BI. In other words, in 2008 we didn't have an audience. Fast-forward three years later and our healthcare practice was booming. Healthcare had leap-frogged ahead in its BI adoption and in a matter of months, a book on healthcare BI seemed like the next right thing to do.

A big thanks to Tom for starting the conversation and re-visiting it until the timing was right. I owe a debt of gratitude to Nancy Dowling, my editor-on-the-side, who kept the quality of my work high. Diane Fiderlein, dear friend and colleague, whose thoroughness and knowledge guided the book from good to great. So many others at Lancet participated in their own time (and some company time) to help make this book a reality. Big thanks go to Paul Sorenson for adding intellectual vigor, and Michael Reid and Neil Schafer for great conversations about architecture and the resultant graphics. I also have to thank all the founders of Lancet for their support and faith: Chris Holtan, Jaime Plante, Rick Thorp, and particularly Randy Mattran, who continues to always expect the absolute best from me; damn that's frustrating! I would be remiss if I didn't mention the Lancet DesignHaus, a team of wildly talented artists who have dedicated themselves to the cause of visualizing data. In their free time they designed all the graphics for this book; Jennifer Maanhardt, Chris Peters, and Mike Erickson—thanks for making my notes and bad sketches look great.

I owe a debt of gratitude to the organizations that agreed to include their case studies in this book. These organizations, and the work that they do in healthcare BI, have continued to inspire not only me but all of our peers too. It's incredibly exciting to be in this industry, and I have these pioneering organizations to thank.

Finally, I have to acknowledge my family. My parents and grandmother, who constantly encouraged me in my incessant need for information and understanding, even at age five. My siblings, whose struggles and experiences with healthcare are detailed in these pages, and most of all, my husband and son. There are no words to thank them for the support that they provide and the patience that they exhibit after my endless hours on the road learning the ins and outs of my industry and then the hours locked in my office writing this book. My appreciation is diminished only by my love for you both.

No matter whose name appears as the "author" it takes a team of people to get a book to its finished state. I am humbled and incredibly fortunate to be able to work with all of you, so I thank you.

Healthcare Business Intelligence

## CHAPTER 1

Business Intelligence

An Introduction

When I tell people what I do for a living they respond one of two ways. First, "Business intelligence, isn't that an oxymoron?" Oh, first time I have heard that! So funny. The second response is: "What?" Complete with a blank stare on their face.

I almost always qualify it with something like "You know, reporting and analytics." That usually seals the deal. It's not completely accurate but in these instances I am okay with good enough.

Many definitions of business intelligence (BI) exist; the most well-known is "The right information to the right person at the right time in the right way." This is my least favorite because it implies a factor of luck. Perhaps the oldest was written by H. P. Luhn in 1958: "The objective of the system is to supply suitable information to support specific activities carried out by individuals, groups, departments, divisions, or even larger units. . . . To that end, the system concerns itself with the admission of acquisition of new information, its dissemination, storage, retrieval, and transmittal to the action points it serves." The one I use most often is: *BI is the integration of data from disparate source systems to optimize business usage and understanding through a user-friendly interface.*

Data warehousing is a companion phrase to BI. The well-documented best practice for BI is to create a data warehouse. A data warehouse is exactly what it sounds like, a place where a lot of data resides. Good data warehouses have a strong organization system, like the card catalogs from libraries of the past. Without that strong organization system, healthcare companies find themselves digging through their data warehouse for data, not an optimized method for certain. To be clear, business intelligence is not an IT (information technology) activity. But it does require support from your IT group for the more technical aspects of data warehousing. We address more of these in Chapter 5.

The truth is that simple definitions don't really do business intelligence justice. True BI, good BI, is an enablement mechanism to provide IT leaders and hospital executives the best information possible to improve their ability to make informed decisions. BI helps organizations go from management by instinct to management by data. BI isn't just a capability, although certainly it provides capabilities; when done well BI can become the life-blood of your organization, providing your organization with key performance indicators that help manage revenue cycle management, quality and safety indicators, or outcomes associated with diabetes management, to name a few. Few healthcare organizations treat BI as life-blood. But as you will see throughout these pages, when they do, the results are nothing short of stellar.

What BI Isn't

BI isn't reporting, it isn't analytics, it isn't data warehousing, and it isn't dashboards. All of these things individually do not make a BI program, but put them together and that is exactly what BI is. Business intelligence enables all of these. BI is greater than the sum of its parts. You may question why BI enables data warehousing, but the truth is that you don't need a data warehouse if you don't intend to analyze data or report from it. BI is an industry and a skill set, but BI isn't the group you go to that will provide you the knowledge or intelligence about your organization. Good BI means putting valuable information at the fingertips of many businesspeople, not just a lucky few.

Is It Really Worth It?

I received a call one early January day. For consultants, those are the calls that are the most intriguing, because usually it means that someone really needs help, contemplated their next steps over the winter holiday, and waited until the new budget year to make the call. This call came the first business day back from break, and the caller was a director of IT. She was looking for an "objective" voice that had knowledge of both tools and BI programs. Two days later I was sitting in her office learning all the details. The most important question she asked me was: "Does anyone really do this? It seems so complicated and hard to find the right resources, is it really worth it?"

The answer is yes; many organizations have done BI and done it well. They have found the proverbial gold at the end of the rainbow, where all the work they did brings them the value from the data that they needed.

Do You Need BI?

If your organization uses data to make decisions then the answer is yes. If your organization *wants* to use data to make decisions then the answer is yes. If your plan is to hire a team of really smart analysts then the answer is no, because BI is meant to deliver information to a broad audience. The degree to which you have to invest and create your BI program is what should vary.

"Do you need BI?" is a great question, and one every person who is in charge of a BI initiative should ask themselves often, and here's why:

- If you don't, someone else will, usually around budget time.
- If you aren't asking then you probably aren't thinking about how to make your program the most relevant for your organization.
- These programs are expensive; between tools, resources, and time they cost money. You have to make sure that you are providing the value that matches the investment. If you aren't, then what are you doing?

Ask yourself these questions at least twice a year, and depending on how your organization is structured, have a prepared statement or a PowerPoint ready when these questions are posed to you by someone else.

Healthcare Information Environment

To "do BI" you will have to organize your data for usage. Odds are, as you read this, your hospital or clinic has data stored somewhere. That data comes from a transactional system like an electronic health record (EHR) or a financial system. The data on its own is not user-friendly for the majority of businesspeople. If the goal of BI is to put better information into many businesspeople's hands you must take the time to organize your data to ensure that it's easy to use and provides the most value. That is where a traditional data warehouse comes in.

When working in healthcare I do make a few modifications to the traditional data structures you see in other books on the topic. For example, the analytics sandbox and audit control sections are critical to healthcare organizations, but maybe not as necessary for retail. Each of them provides a method to allow your more sophisticated analysts access to the data that is granular. The analytic sandbox provides your analysts a "play space" to create predictive models that can help you adjust staffing in your emergency department without an impact to regulatory reporting. The audit control environment (ACE) provides a one-stop-shop for both internal and external auditors to see the data and the path the data took to validate your approach for anything from JCAHO (the Joint Commission for the Accreditation of Healthcare Organizations) reviews to medical records reviews for public health documentation.

The first thing you should know about your data environment is that it is unique to your organization and should be created based on the needs and wants of your hospital or health plan. As you construct your information environment, important key criteria need to be kept in mind. These environments are built to optimize stability and data usage for your organization. Some methods of shortcutting the process exist, but few deliver the capabilities that are promised during the sales cycle. We review these methods in Chapter 5, but for now let's look at the baseline healthcare information environment that I recommend.

Let's start at the beginning, or in this case, on the left side of Figure 1.1. The source systems in healthcare do vary, but they generally follow two categories: Clinical and Financial. In theory, anything that has data can be a source (e.g., Excel), but as you consider what you bring into your data warehouse you need to ask yourself a basic question: "Yes, you can, but *should* you?" Every industry is buckling under the weight of data, prompting interest in "the Cloud." But not all data is equal, only data that provide valuable insights should be stored in your data warehouse.

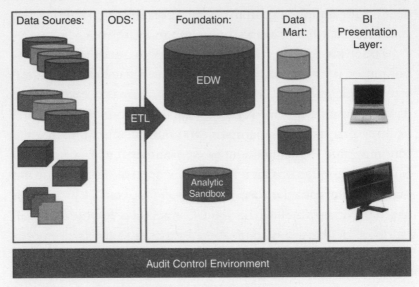

FIGURE 1.1 Healthcare Information Environment

The next step in the environment is the staging area, often referred to as the *operational data store*. Named for the type of data that generally appears, for healthcare we find that the staging area provides an important two-stage function. The first is to isolate activity against your transactional system. In other words, you don't want your EHR performance to slow down so that you can run a report, and staging areas help provide that buffer. The second function is to maintain a completely untouched version of the data that can be used if there is a data load failure. This prevents the need to go back to your transactional systems (EHR or financial system) to pull the data again. This also protects the transactional system. We take a copy of this data and store it, untouched, in the audit control tables. These tables enable support for the internal and external audits that are routinely done in healthcare. Although not necessary, these control tables make audits much easier to manage because all of the required data and supporting documentation needed for audits (e.g., transformation scripts that outline the changes that were made to the data) are included.

The next section is the extract, transform, and load, or ETL, portion of the healthcare information environment. ETL is absolutely critical for healthcare. In its raw form most healthcare data is unusable for the average businessperson. The "transformation" part of ETL is the application of business rules so we can aggregate things like encounters and deduplicate provider and patient records. Once the business rules are applied we place this data into an organized set of data tables within the data warehouse itself where the most granular level of data exists, such as the claim level or patient level. The function of a data warehouse is to aggregate the most granular data up into summary level data to improve the ability to use the data. For example, in its most granular form a claims record can have many rows (think about this in the context of Excel). Each row may represent a different status of the same claim, such as submitted, paid, reversed, or rejected. Most claims go through many different statuses before it's considered a "final paid" claim. If the average businessperson is only interested in the percentage of rejected claims, then having to go through this granular data is time consuming. The organization of your data warehouse removes the need for a businessperson to have to do that by aggregating (in this case summing) the number of rejected claims for a specific time period or place based on business rules.

Within this environment an analytic sandbox can also exist. These sandboxes are the "play space" for your analysts and they should not allow the average businessperson access. These sandboxes give analysts a chance to test models and create new business rules or functionality without exposing the activity to everyone. This allows for innovation using data. As we move right in Figure 1.1 you see the data mart section. Data marts represent logical subject areas, such as claims or encounters, any subject area that you report on frequently; data marts are created to improve performance (response time of reports). In other words, most of your standard reports will access data contained in these data marts. This is not a required method, but if you know that you will have a high degree of usage of reports, these logical subject areas are quite helpful in managing the overall performance of the system.

Finally, we have the BI presentation layer. This presentation layer represents the BI products that you have bought (e.g., MicroStrategy, Cognos, Tableau, SAS) to allow your businesspeople access to the data. This would include products that provide reports, dashboards, or even ad hoc analysis to all users of the data. I will make a somewhat controversial statement and say that your BI presentation layer will likely have multiple tools. Some tools are better at certain things than others, and if you have a strong analytic component of your BI program, your standard BI product will likely not meet all of your needs.

Every BI program is different because every organization is different—this is not a one size fits all. If you've seen one BI program you have seen one BI program. Critical similarities, such as the need for a data warehouse, ETL (in some form), and a method of report distribution exist, but the rest is the art of good BI.

The art of BI is probably the most difficult thing to master. It is often the function most overlooked by organizations. I have seen hundreds of BI programs, and each one is different, but the ones that have considered the "softer" side of delivering valuable information to their businesspeople are successful. They have considered what it takes, who it takes, and haven't compromised on quality, or backed down on the need for good architectural standards. They are a testament to what good BI programs *do*. Good programs have strong BI leadership that is aligned and empowered. They have a strong and dedicated staff, they don't go for the "easy" button, and they understand that the foundation of everything starts with data modeling.

Data Modeling

I have struggled many times to explain or define data modeling to a businessperson. When business leaders are trying to decide whether they should invest in this thing called a *data model*, where the deliverable, at least from their perspective, is a drawing, it isn't that complicated. But when they get down to what data modeling can do for their BI deployment and how it does it, it gets tougher.

Most people understand the concept of data hierarchies, and the idea that some data cannot be summed. Much of that understanding is the foundation of data modeling. When you do data modeling right, you define the hierarchal nature of the data. A great example is time: Year, Quarter, Month, Week, Day, Hour. For most healthcare organizations you have some type of organizational hierarchy such as Department, Unit, and Floor. The other part of data modeling is identifying the "facts" and "dimensions." Simply, the things that can be summed and the dimensions are attributes of the facts. For example: A dimension of a patient or member is their unique identifier, so you can't sum that. You can sum the total number of patients or members, which is a fact. The vast majority of data modeling is simply organizing your data in the appropriate hierarchies, facts, and dimensions.

The art of data modeling is to know when to do what, and how to create the relationships between these. In healthcare the relationships in our data are complex; in data warehousing we call it a *many-to-many*, which happens over and over again (think about the relationship between a patient, physician, diagnostic code, member, address, etc.).

I will stop here, at the risk of getting too much into the detail to confuse the point. The point is, data modeling for healthcare is complex and requires a special skill set. We discuss this further in Chapter 5.

The Don'ts

Much of this book focuses on what you *should* do, but here are four things you absolutely should not, under any circumstances, do:

1. *Never* make a consultant the leader of your program. Yes, I said it. And, yes, I am a consultant. But for much longer I was a BI practitioner in an organization a lot like yours, and I have made this mistake. Here's the simple reason why this will never work—consultants are not employees. Sure, consultants want your program to succeed but their reasons for that are not aligned with what is best for *your* organization—they are aligned with what is best for *the consultant's* organization. Consultants will strive to be kept around and will find ways to ensure that happens. It doesn't matter how much you like them or trust them, and it doesn't mean that they set out to mislead; it just means that you are not aligned with each other, and that is never a good thing. Instead, invest in a BI leader who is on your payroll and reports up to the executive who has the most on the line for a successful BI program.

2. Don't ignore or forget about your staff. This could probably be said for any program, not just BI. But at the end of the day BI is your intellectual property (IP), and the only way you get good IP is to have really smart, dedicated people thinking about your business and the data. Few things are as powerful as a highly internally motivated staff that will do whatever it takes to get the job done the right way.

3. If it sounds too good to be true, it is. Didn't our mothers teach us this? Well, please forgive me, my vendor friends, but when a vendor tells you that you can install and plug in your data and be up and running in a few days, take that with a giant grain of salt. Yes, *technically* this is true, but just because you *can* doesn't always mean you *should*. What you will get are some reports, and that can help get some executive support, but what you won't get are the things that are the hallmarks of good BI programs: things like a reuseable data warehouse, good data-quality processes, and automated ETL scripts.

4. Never de-emphasize the importance of a good data model. If I had a dime for every time I have seen this I would be rich. This is highly correlated to the "easy" button phenomenon. Again, sorry my vendor friends, but you usually cannot buy a 100 percent ready-to-go data model. If you do, please know that the value comes in the customization (yes, customizing a prebuilt template), so it can jump-start your program; it just won't get you over the finish line.

If you have decided that you need BI and are ready to start on this journey, here are the hallmarks of good BI programs. They:

- Have good leaders who are employees.
- Have solid executive sponsorship.
- Are willing, or have, invested in the right tools and people to get the job done.
- Are committed to data governance.
- Focus on all aspects of delivering BI.
- Maintain excellent communication out to the business community during any build cycle.

If you do these things, you are well on your way. The rest of this book is dedicated to each of these hallmarks of BI programs, referred to as the *Tenets of Healthcare BI*. If you have started your program and already have some of these, you can skip to the chapters that will be most helpful to you. If you are starting from scratch, you'll benefit from reading this book from cover to cover and joining our online collaborative community for further discussions.

## CHAPTER 2

The Tenets of Healthcare BI

N ow that you understand what business intelligence (BI) is, and you have decided that BI is a part of your organization's future, you have to understand the BI perspective that is unique to healthcare. There are things, common things, which every BI program needs: a data warehouse, data governance, data integration, and so on. But there are other dimensions that are critical to healthcare BI that don't necessarily pertain to other industries, or at least not to the same degree.

In the healthcare industry, patient care data creates the need for BI, and rightly so. Most healthcare organizations are deeply concerned about quality, effectiveness, and value. Each aspect of healthcare has data points that help organizations determine the benchmark and measure the relative improvement. Many of the regulatory requirements imposed on both payers and providers today are aimed at some aspect of quality, effectiveness, and value of patient care.

In order for a BI program to be influential in a healthcare organization, you must ensure that you have the ability to report, monitor, and measure quality, effectiveness, and value in patient care. Alignment is important to ensure that the content delivered by the BI program matches what the organization needs. The concepts of quality, effectiveness, and value apply broadly to the healthcare industry as a whole, so your organization may have others, or may not address one of these. The concepts will still apply, and you can adapt them to fit your organization's needs.

As we consider the key aspects of quality, effectiveness, and value in conjunction with our definition of BI, we have loosely outlined the tenets of healthcare BI. Our accepted definition of BI in Chapter 1 says: "BI is the integration of data from disparate source systems to optimize business usage and understanding through a user-friendly interface." We must define healthcare BI in a way that allows us to create a program that will support the measurement of quality, effectiveness, and value but also addresses the areas that are critical to success within a healthcare organization. Therefore, our definition of healthcare BI must be: "The integration of data from clinical systems, financial systems, and other disparate data sources into a data warehouse that requires a set of validated data to address the concepts of clinical quality, effectiveness of care, and value for business usage." The rest of this book addresses the finer details of these five tenets as shown in Figure 2.1.

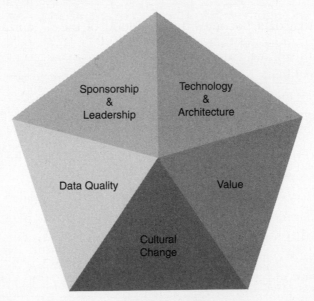

FIGURE 2.1 The Five Tenets of Healthcare BI

The Tenets

Data quality: It could be said that data quality is important to any industry, but it is absolutely critical to healthcare BI—no one dies if a retail report misrepresents inventory in an end-cap—so it lands in our number one spot as the first tenet of healthcare BI. Perhaps more than any other tenet, quality data helps drive trust and user adoption of the program. Data quality is relative, and having high-quality data doesn't mean that your data is 100 percent accurate, because after all, what is accurate? There are many aspects of data quality that we will cover, including the concepts of data governance, data profiling, and data certification.

Leadership and sponsorship: Some of the most successful healthcare BI programs started because one person was absolutely passionate about the difference data can make to an organization. Long-term sponsorship requires full engagement and a knowledgeable staff. It means that the organization isn't just giving some time to it, but is dedicating, fueling, and insisting that data becomes the life-blood of the organization. It is a leadership activity but doesn't always require a person in a traditional leadership role in your organization. We review the different levels of sponsorship and what it takes to support your sponsor for the long term.

Technology and architecture: To be clear, business intelligence is not an IT activity. But investing in the best practices associated with data modeling; extract, transform, and load (ETL); and solid BI applications will ensure performance and scalability. Data modeling doesn't get much more complicated than in healthcare. Ensuring the right data model will allow your program to flourish without having to "change the tire at 60 miles per hour." Few industries have the fragmented and messy data that healthcare does. Healthcare data is fragmented, coming from many different systems (electronic health records

15

[EHRs], financial systems, etc.) and more often than not the data is driven from contextual information or data such as nurse notes. As a reference to our first tenet, ETL is the only way to make data usable to the average end-user. We must ensure that the baseline IT-specific activities are addressed to allow time to focus on much of the other work in BI.

Value: Every aspect of healthcare BI must provide value. Healthcare organizations are overburdened and understaffed, particularly when it comes to data. There is no room for theoretical exercises or interesting investigations (that comes after you are well established). To get started, you must focus where BI can provide the organization with the most value. Much of what we will discuss from a value perspective will concern the delivery of reports, dashboards, and ad hoc analysis. We will address how to best bring your business users with you, such as training and providing support. Finally, we will evaluate your user-base and determine how to best deliver value to each group.

Cultural change: Collaboration is the glue that holds a good BI team together. Ask any BI professional and you'll hear that much of the challenge isn't bad data quality or poor tools, but politics and organizational dynamics. I have worked with enough hospitals to tell you that our healthcare organizations are as susceptible to the pitfalls of human nature as any other organization; some may even be worse than average. I was once told by a research assistant that I had a diplomatic way of solving issues. You will need as much diplomacy as a UN ambassador as you start this journey. You will encounter naysayers, "me-too'ers," a glut of "I don't have the time" folks, and "just give me the data" responses. I have been in meetings with physicians, nurses, administrators, and finance gurus, and I have heard it all. You'll need the courage to stay above it all, and continue to support a collaborative approach among all the stakeholders.

Bringing these five tenets together creates a fully functioning BI program that's optimized for success in a healthcare organization.

Data Quality

Data quality by itself could be the subject of a long book. The importance of data quality really can't be underestimated in healthcare. It not only drives our ability to make decisions based on data but drives end-user adoption of BI programs. Few things kill BI programs faster than bad data.

It is important to recognize that there is no such thing as 100 percent clean data. That statement will disturb a few of you. I know this because when I make this statement in presentations throughout the country, one person in the audience makes an audible gasp. This statement is meant to be provocative, but it's also reality. Data is flawed from creation, and our ability to change that would require herculean efforts. But just because we don't seek out 100 percent clean data doesn't mean we cannot strive for a fully validated and certified data set. To do our work well, we must strive for the best data possible.

A number of years ago I was working with a health plan to implement a business intelligence product. I had acquired this customer from a previous product manager and had been at the implementation for more than two years. Most of our clients implemented in six to nine months, so I wondered, "Why is it taking so long?" The answer was data quality. They decided that 100 percent data quality was their goal, and two years later they were still working on data quality questions on every cell of a 10-million-plus-row database. A large team of analysts and businesspeople did the data profiling and then tracked down every errant entry. Once investigated, many of those errant entries resulted in a process change to the organization. The effort was admirable, but flawed. The final cost of the project was staggering, and just a few weeks after going live its data was no longer 100 percent accurate.

The idea of tackling data quality seems overwhelming to many. Data comes in torrents every day, week, or month, depending on how often you bring it over. Determining what represents high-quality data in your organization, and then deciding what to do about it, can be a BI manager's worst nightmare. The good news is that's where data governance comes in. Data quality and data governance are forever entwined. Data governance is a process more than a product. It requires that your business users of the data become owners of the data and take ownership over the data to define it, and then manage it within those parameters. The only real way to assess whether you have high-quality data is to have a data governance function that will tell you what high quality means.

Data governance administration is not the glamorous part of data quality (assuming there is a glamorous part), but it's important to ensure that you have a method to keep the data governance function running as smoothly as possible. Data governance administration entails the creation and management of the content created by the data stewards as well as the data governance committees. Data stewards are the guardians of good quality data in your organization, and we explore them in depth in Chapter 4.

To some organizations, high-quality data means nothing more than pulling data from the source systems and plopping it down—what some data warehouse consultants refer to as "suck and plunk." For others, as I described earlier, it's nothing less than ensuring that the data is 100 percent clean. When I work with clients who are just getting started, I always recommend that they start with a data governance council and one question: How much data quality is good enough data quality? Not all of the data is there for clinical decisions. Not all of the data is there for financial decisions. First determine the threshold for quality and then modify the BI processes to meet that threshold.

We have addressed the data quality once the data lands in the data warehouse (as part of the ETL process), but what about the data quality that comes directly out of the transactional systems, where our data lives? Data profiling, the method of analyzing data against parameters to determine if it fits the accepted profile, can be an incredibly powerful tool in your fight for high-quality data. Even if you have a team of analysts who know your data like the back of their hands, data profiling quantifies all of the issues and helps the team know where the worst trouble spots are. When I was working on my master's degree my first step was always data profiling, although I didn't call it that. My degree program trained me how to use data that already existed, but that meant I had to know what I was dealing with, warts and all. To do that, I would run frequencies on the data. Doing this provided me with the mean, median, mode, minimum, and maximum for each field of data. This type of base-level understanding of data helps an organization to identify data that is inherently inaccurate, but more importantly, it shows where you can apply the business rules to ensure that the data that lands in your data warehouse is ready for use.

It might be important at this point to make a statement about usage. If your intention is to hire a whole bunch of really smart data analysts, then a data warehouse and BI program is not the most cost-effective method of getting the analysts the data they need to do their job. Data warehouses are created to ensure a broader user-base. If you don't intend on investing in data quality for a warehouse to provide a broader user-base with the data that they can use, then there's no reason to create a warehouse—a team of analysts can work just fine. However, keep in mind that data warehouse and BI programs are built for scalability and usage; a team of analysts is not. What works today with five data analysts may not function efficiently two years from now when data volumes have grown three times. In addition, if you are not applying a broadly accepted set of definitions to the data (such as business rules to define "bed days"), then each of your analysts is probably coming up with his or her own. That means that you will be sitting around the boardroom with three different answers to the same question.

Data profiling allows you to understand your data in a different way. Running the descriptive statistics (i.e., mean, median, mode) is helpful to assess the mess so you can apply the business rules in the warehouse. If you have no intention of fixing the data then it's best that you don't allow access to the warehouse to the average end-user. Allowing access to a larger user-base implies that your organization is looking to put data in end-users' hands to broaden the ability of people throughout your organization to make better decisions.

Metadata Management

Other aspects of data management drive data quality, or perhaps the perception of data quality. Metadata management is closely related to data governance in that the decisions and actions of the data governance function must be played out in the metadata. But before I get too far down into the idiosyncrasies of metadata, I have to answer an important question: What is metadata? The most popular definition is: it's data about data. To me, that definition is less than useful. The analogy that best suits metadata is the card catalogs and Dewey Decimal System. Long before we used computers to find and read books, you would go directly to the card catalog to look up your book choice. The system included a method of looking up books by author's name. You simply went alphabetically until you found it. Then it would include a code, something like 123.11, designating a category and location. Then you would write that down and go find your book. A modern example of this type of simple metadata is how Ikea stores and distributes their furniture. There again you write down a code and use it to find the location of the chair you want.

The best way to consider metadata is to understand how data is created, stored, and defined. There are actually three types of metadata. The structural metadata, which is the data about how the content is created, is not really about data at all since the data doesn't exist yet. For the purposes of BI this type of metadata isn't really useful, but it does exist in the originating application (i.e., your EHR). The technical metadata is the data about where the content exists. In our case, that is the data warehouse. This technical metadata includes things like table name and column. At this point, this metadata is reported as this: "ENCOUNTER_TBL.ENCOUNTER_ID" and it can go on for quite a while if you have a complicated data model. As the average end-user would have no idea what this means, we have created business metadata. Business metadata includes all the data that applies to how end-users want to see or understand the data. For example, if we are calculating our average length of stay (ALOS), we will include the definition of ALOS: Total number of patient days divided by the number of admissions and discharges over a specified time period. Then we would include the impacted tables, such as UNIQUE_PT, ADMISSION_ CNT & DISCHARGE_CNT, and finally the timetables (such as day, week, and month of year). The business metadata is the most important aspect of metadata because it helps the end-users understand how data is defined and calculated.

Now that we understand what metadata is, we can discuss how to manage it. Management of metadata is important because it allows end-users exposure to the common definitions of the data. To do that you must assign someone responsibility for taking what is decided by the data governance function and finalizing it into the metadata repository. Sometimes that's just a really big spreadsheet, and other times it's a separate software system or part of your BI Presentation layer. Regardless of how you tackle the software aspect of metadata, it's important that you ensure that the process aspect of metadata is well documented and understood. But most importantly, you must provide business metadata to your end-users so they understand the data they are using.

Leadership and Sponsorship

As an employee in a large corporation, it's easy to recognize the value of sponsorship. Frankly, few large-scale efforts get done in a corporation unless someone in a suit with a door is backing up your project. You will need this backing to gain momentum and legitimacy. That's the positive side of sponsorship. The negative side is about protecting yourself. One of my bosses explained to me once, "CYA, Laura. If it goes south, it's on them and not you. That's the only way you can survive." That boss shall remain nameless, for obvious reasons.

Let me tell you about a time when lack of sponsorship really took its toll. On a cold January day, the first week back from the holiday haze, we received a call at the office. The request was simple: Did we have anyone who could come in and do a BI product assessment. The client had two BI products and wanted—needed—to consolidate. I was in the client's office the next day. On the surface, the request was so easy I could have probably done it in a few hours, but then she closed the door and told me the rest of the story.

Three years prior to this meeting, my client was in an enviable position. The organization had a fully integrated, well-modeled, and highly popular data warehouse. The manager (at the time) didn't feel like he needed a high degree of sponsorship because he had been incredibly successful without one. He never took the time to educate the leadership on the value of the team, the role it played in the organization, or the complexities associated with the work. As the organization grew, the business decided it was time for a new and updated financial system. Without even a nod to BI, they purchased (lock, stock, and barrel) a fully integrated application stack that included a black-box (supposedly industry specific) data model, front-end tool, and packaged ETL scripts. The BI manager attempted to tell them the error of their ways to no avail. He left nine months later, exhausted from the fight.

As I sat in the office of the person now responsible for the deployment, she recognized where it had all fallen apart. She conceded that the lock, stock, and barrel product, while perhaps good in other settings, didn't fit their business and had failed—miserably. The supposed "product consolidation" was really more of an effort to bring competing groups together for the common good, including a newly promoted VP who was now their executive sponsor.

What this client lacked was a sponsor who understood the ramifications of the decision. Good sponsorship is not a check-box activity. It takes work to identify the right person, convince him or her of the importance, and then educate him or her on the key aspects of BI and data warehousing. There are three levels of sponsorship: traditional, influencer, and grassroots. Each of these levels can have a different perspective on sponsoring the program. Only the traditional and influencer levels could have the potential to budget for the activity, but they could also have the most to lose without it. The grassroots efforts feel the pain of the lack of cohesion every day; their support helps clarify the value to someone who can support the initiative financially. This is why leadership and sponsorship are different; you need people who understand the value and are willing to put their money where their mouth is.

The traditional executive sponsor is the one with the "right" title and the checkbook. Generally speaking these are the C-level executives and vice presidents of the organization. But the challenge is that they have a million things on their plate, and it's hard for you to be heard above the fray. So when you walk into their office, they have not spent any time thinking about your project. To prepare for the possible directions the conversation may take, you will need to have a fair amount of "back-pocket" content, such as examples of possible dashboards, anecdotes from other organizations that have been successful, or even an action plan to get going. Keep in mind that they often have to deal with every aspect of managing an organization and you should try to predict their concerns and questions. Anytime you go in front of an executive you need to do your research. Spend some time getting to know the organization in a way you hadn't considered before. Talk with department heads of the organization and work to understand their daily needs and struggles. You will look like a rock-star supernova if you are ready with anything the executive fires at you.

As you are talking with the department heads, keep in mind that you are never really done looking for a sponsor. The other type of sponsor is the "Influencer"; this person generally has a leadership title and is well respected among the senior leadership. The influencer is often the voice of reason that many leaders will listen to. The influencer can be your main connection to the executive sponsor. Keep in mind that the arguments to win over the influencer are different from the arguments to win over the executive. The influencers are looking for the projects that will make them even more indispensable in the eyes of the leadership, or even better, make them seem like prophets.

Finally, you have the grassroots effort. Although not technically a "sponsor," the grassroots build-up of the project and program will be a short-term loss but a long-term gain. This grassroots effort is exactly what it sounds like; you build up enthusiasm and interest in the average end-user. They become your cheerleaders and start to ask their bosses about the project and when things will get started. They'll start telling other people, and eventually it will come around back to you when someone asks you about "this new BI thing." Then, and only then, do you know that your grassroots efforts will be successful.

Sponsorship ensures success. If you have addressed all three of these areas of sponsorship, even if you move on to bigger and better projects, the program will continue because a team of people is responsible for the leadership of the program.

BI programs are highly political. BI is like the UN of your organization. It brings everyone together for shared decision making and responsibility. Sometimes that means good things like using data to better determine process improvement efforts for Lean Six Sigma. Other times, it has to make really tough decisions about vendors, or worse, employees. Some people will be on your side and other people won't (maybe because they didn't think of it first). Good sponsorship across these three dimensions means that you are not alone fighting the good fight.

The support of these key stakeholders is critical to the long-term success of the function. At the end of the day, they hold the purse strings. One of the most consequential things you can do to gain executive support is to clearly articulate a vision and a return on investment (ROI). Several topics are controversial in the BI industry and ROI is one of them. Many BI professionals will tell you that you can't get to an ROI because many of the benefits are soft and immeasurable. A "hard" ROI is a challenge in BI, but that doesn't mean we can dismiss it. We owe it to our leadership to put our money where our mouth is. If you can't do that, the likelihood of your BI function flourishing is highly unlikely.

One of the major drivers of ROI is end-user adoption. If users aren't adopting, then you won't be able to attribute better and faster decision making to your BI work. Creating a thorough and frequently delivered training program and support function will keep your users humming along. But if your data lacks the quality that users expect, this will challenge your success.

Communication is an important part of the BI program and falls under sponsorship. Ensuring that good information gets out to the entire organization can certainly drive value, but it really serves to reassure your sponsors that activities are getting done. To do this, I recommend a marketing plan. Marketing plans help you plan all of the activities associated with promoting what your team is doing to deliver value to the organization. Sometimes it can feel like a full-time job just communicating to end-users, so having a good method of scheduling and documenting each communication can help a great deal.

Technology and Architecture

Memory is a funny thing. Research on the topic of memory and recall has shown that emotional experiences are permanently etched into our brain. Many of my stories here were part of the run-of-the-mill BI work I have done over the past decade. Healthcare BI work isn't the most emotional work; much of it is just questions about indexing and data quality. But sometimes, the phone rings in the middle of the night, like it did back in 2001. I had been working for a payer organization that had grown by acquisition. The area I worked in was in charge of a new line of services we provided to pharmaceutical companies. The service provided phone-based nursing services to individuals taking an adherence-challenged medication. It was one of those medications where the cure was worse than the disease. It had the ability to do things like change the color of your irises. Our job was to deliver disease-management type services as well as be on the other end to document adverse events.

To be clear, this wasn't part of our normal business model. In fact, it was just one of many changes that had occurred to the team over the previous 12 months. Many on the team had requested that we slow down and take the time to assess how the data was being collected and stored, but time wasn't on our side. Then the call came in at 11 p.m. on a Tuesday night. The analyst simply said that she missed a join (a relationship in the data specific to how you write a query). It seemed like an innocuous thing to miss, but when you are responsible for reporting adverse events to the FDA, it was anything but innocuous.

That join meant that we missed reporting more than 10 documented adverse events to the FDA. That's a significant number when the total population taking this drug is only in the low thousands. The following weeks were filled with meetings with lawyers and marking all documentation with "Privileged and Confidential." We were investigated by the FDA, the client threatened a multimillion dollar lawsuit, and the pharmaceutical services we provided were shuttered within months. Finally, the postmortem analysis of the disaster revealed what most of us on the team had known within hours of that late-night call: the data model was not optimized for usage.

For certain, this is an extreme case. It was highly emotional. I had never worked so hard, or been so scared, in my professional life before or since. (It is funny how FDA investigations and multimillion-dollar lawsuits can do that to you.) It is the best example of the importance of your data model, and what can go wrong when you don't invest in one.

When business leaders are trying to decide whether they should invest in this thing called a data model, where the deliverable, at least from their perspective, is a drawing, I tell them this story. Data modeling is more than just a drawing of boxes and lines, but provides the framework for how your organization will use the data. Now and forever, every one of my clients will be counseled on the importance of a data model.

Data modeling isn't a one-time effort. Your data and the business surrounding it changes all the time—and so should your data model. That's actually one of the hardest things about data modeling, the constant change. So in sum, it's difficult, it changes all the time, and it requires a specialized skill set. I can't emphasize the importance of data modeling enough; it is absolutely the foundation on which you build your program.

BI and IT: Frienemies

Technology and architecture is where traditional IT meets business intelligence. These functions are really important to keeping your program running smoothly. The IT team will be critical to the care and feeding of the environment that your end-users will be accessing. If the server needs to be maintained or upgraded, or you need someone to fix the server if it crashes, this team is the team to do it.

Much of what happens in this department won't even hit the radar screen of the average BI user and that's exactly what you want. If you don't have direct managerial responsibility for this group, it's a good idea to put some service level agreements (SLAs) in place to ensure a timely response to issues. Some of these functions can be "outsourced" to your internal

IT team. Examples of activities that will be managed by your IT team:

- Supporting the BI infrastructure and processes
- Server and web administration
- Application architecture
- Metadata repository
- Application development and management
- Usage tracking
- Customer support

Part of the BI team's responsibility is to determine the level of system availability that you require. High-availability means that the hardware and software are available 24 hours a day and seven days a week. If that's really what your end-users expect, then that's what you request from your IT team. This decision will impact how your IT needs to support the BI deployment, and will change how you write your SLAs.

Application architecture is the landscape of all the products that your organization uses that require hardware. This can include your BI products, but it can include other products as well. This team will ensure that all of the applications are on stable platforms and ensure availability. This special type of architecture associated with applications ensures that the system takes the best advantage of what you have in the hardware.

ETL is the mechanism most BI efforts use to get data out of the source systems and into an integrated data warehouse. ETL is a more technical function and has impacts to both technology and architecture. More complex than a simple "dump and load," which many of us do, good ETL offers us the opportunity to not only apply business rules (the "T" in ETL), but also introduce quality checks into the data. ETL is critically important to the success of healthcare BI programs because it's the primary and most significant opportunity we have to prepare data for usage by end-users. If your team is a team full of data analysts, that's one thing, but if your intention is to improve end-user self-service you must spend time reviewing the data, aggregating it (so that one encounter is aggregated from its original 217 rows of data), and loading it into your data model that has been created with scalability and usability in mind.

Support Calls

Whether or not you are prepared for them, support calls will happen. Users are logging into your system every day of the week, many of them from different locations. If you plan to have some level of customer support in place to manage these calls, your users will perceive a better level of service and end-user adoption will be more successful. It's unlikely that establishing a support plan alone will save a struggling BI program. If the data are "wrong" and the performance is poor, no amount of support will help you, but everything else being equal, support programs tell your end-users that you are serious about making their experience with the product positive.

In your plan, create three levels of support. The nature of the call will determine how quickly you need to respond. Generally speaking, unless your BI program is driving your business, Level-One calls are rare. Level-One calls are the calls that require intervention within eight business hours (i.e., the same day the call is placed, for example, when the server goes down). If your BI program really runs your business then questionable data quality might become a Level-One call. For the rest of us, that's probably a Level-Two call that can be managed within two business days (or three, depending on how forgiving your end-users are). Finally Level-Three calls are for reports not running, or strange fonts or spacing. Believe me, these things happen.

Providing Value

A few years ago I was working with a provider organization just starting its BI program. It had purchased a BI platform and then management realized that they needed to decide where to begin using it. For this organization, the starting point was easy. It had grown through acquisition, and although that provided challenges in itself, the biggest problem was that the leaders were trying to manage the whole enterprise through a series of spreadsheets. These spreadsheets took hours and hours each month to complete. They were also error prone, as one fat-fingering mishap could cost the organization valuable time and a potentially flawed decision.

It was decided that the first spreadsheet the BI team would work to replace would be the management key performance indicators (KPIs). The KPIs had already been identified and defined. We knew where the data came from, and how messy it was. All we needed to do was integrate the data from the disparate source systems and put it together in the BI interface product.

Approximately six months later we had replaced the spreadsheet with a new visually appealing dashboard. It had thresholds and gauges that indicated to management when bed days were lower than forecasted, or when staffing was higher or lower than optimal. The value the dashboard provided to the organization was immeasurable. It kick-started the entire BI program that continues today. One of the smartest moves the organization made at the outset was deciding not to boil the ocean. We picked one project that would deliver value, we created a solid foundation that provided room for growth, but we focused all of our efforts on that first deliverable.

Six months does seem like a long time to wait to produce something. But when you are just getting started, and this work is new to you and your team, six months is a reasonable expectation. Once this first big effort is done, though, development time for subsequent projects should diminish considerably.

From the "starting small" approach to the design of data, all of these factors influence the amount and perception of value. The way we define value in this context is the method and processes required to deliver information to end-users to improve decision-making ability. We need to cover many aspects of value; we address a few of the key ones here.

Training

To ensure value as perceived by end-users, be sure that you offer training. Although it's not usually the first thing that comes to mind when you start your BI program, it has the potential of making or breaking end-user adoption. Today's BI tools are easy to use compared to even five years ago, but that doesn't mean that users will have an easy time adapting. Even if they are used to using BI tools, a major upgrade or change to a new platform can really challenge end-users. It's best to be proactive and have a thorough training program up and running the week before you go live. Don't make it any earlier than that because people will forget, and even with one week it's good to have a "sandbox" environment—a place that allows users to experience the BI platform until it goes into production.

It's important to have different delivery methods for your training program. Use products like Camtasia to create an online training program that users can log into anytime to find lessons on the simple tasks like logging in, changing preferences, selecting dates, and so on. Creating an online program will reduce the calls to your team. Offer in-person courses frequently during the month of a release and repeat them at least once a month from then on. Create a set of printable documentation for those folks who just have to see the written word on paper. Try to remember that most of your end-users will only log into the system once a month. In the meantime they have a job to do that fills up most of their memory bank. Their approach to the BI tool is like your approach to your 401(k) website; you do it when you need the data to make better decisions.

Business Analysts

Business analytics, or business analysts, are an integral part of delivering value. First, it's important to clarify what I mean by business analysts. Refer to Chapter 1 where we define BI; it's clear that BI is an enablement mechanism. Therefore, you don't go to your BI group to learn about your business. Your BI group should be enabling your business teams to do that. Business analysts are the people who document requirements from the business and translate them for consumption by IT. They are not "analysts" in the sense of analyzing data. To be clear, for the remainder of the book I refer to those roles as data analysts.

Data visualization is a term that probably wasn't muttered often in the average organization a few years back. Conceptually, the idea is to take the mountain of data confronting us and turn it into something that can easily be consumed visually. The advancements in BI tools in the past few years have resulted in the ability to easily produce sophisticated data visualizations. From web to mobile, making sure that your data is easily consumed is a clear way to provide value.

Now that we have a clear understanding of what business analysts do, we understand that their role is particularly important and challenging. They are the bridge between technical and business. The closer you can get these two concepts together, the better off you will be. Often, "requirements" get lost in translation, where business users articulate their needs in a straightforward but nonspecific way (such as "give me the data") and IT users are looking for something specific (such as where the data can be found, how it should be transformed, and the frequency in which it should be displayed). Without BAs that gap means rework, and rework means longer timelines and more money. Investing in BAs may save your organization money in the long run.

Project Management

Project management provides a methodology to manage resources and tasks toward a common end-goal. Having a method for managing all of the activities involved in a BI implementation and rollout is important. The well-documented methods of good project management are what we are looking for. We need a method of planning and managing many tasks. It doesn't matter whether you subscribe to Project Management Professional methods (PMP), Project Management Institute methods (PMI), Waterfall, Iterative, or Agile methods—that is not really at issue. Besides having a well-accepted project management method throughout your organization, you also must have a way of managing to milestones and assessing whether you are on time. Consistency with rolling out content is an important aspect of delivering value. If you are not constantly finding ways to get the job done and getting new content in the end-users' hands, then you are not delivering value.

Planning

Beyond project management, you will want to do some planning in the form of road maps. Road maps are an excellent way to look out onto the landscape and plan your course for the next 18 months. This longer-term view requires a vision of what BI can provide to the organization and a path to get you there. Road maps should outline your BI journey. As you do this, make sure that you leave room for later modifications. That old saying about "the best laid plans..." applies to road maps as well. The real value of a road map is as a tool to help you articulate to supporters and dissenters alike what the program will be delivering and when.

Cultural Implications

The final tenet is the cultural implication of BI programs. Initially, I didn't make this a tenet. I've always felt that it was important but I wasn't sure it was something that had to be addressed as a primary ingredient for success. As I got further and further along I recognized that although it's the most "fluffy" of all the tenets, it is the one that after all is said and done can make or break your program.

Change is hard, and pushing an organization from management by instinct to management by data introduces all sorts of challenges. If you understand the impact that the culture has on the change, and you have a plan to manage that change, the transition will be smoother for everyone.

In Chapter 7 we review a series of assessments that help you determine how prepared your organization is to adopt this type of change. Chapter 7 also guides you in how to tackle the results in a step-wise approach to improve your organization's ability to adapt to managing with data.

Seeking Equilibrium

What you may have noticed by now is how interconnected the BI world is. One of the challenges associated with this work is trying to decide what to do when. Don't worry; we'll go into that later. But what's important to understand is that what you do has an impact on other aspects of BI. Thinking about it

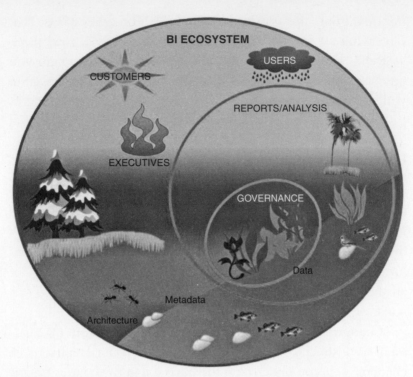

FIGURE 2.2 BI Ecosystem

this way reminded me of my fourth-grade science class and the ecosystem (see Figure 2.2).

We must seek out equilibrium in all aspects of BI work. If one area in the ecosystem gets out of balance the other areas will compensate for it until it can come back in-line, or one of the other areas fails. Frankly, if you were to do an analysis of the reasons why BI programs fail, 9 times out of 10 it could be traced back to a false sense of equilibrium within the ecosystem. It's important to remember from this perspective that the ecosystem in its entirety is your organization. The BI program will live and die within the confines of your organization.

These tenets are the key to the successful creation and continued survival of your healthcare BI program. All the tenets are important but not every aspect of every tenet needs to be completed during the first month. As you create your BI program, you will keep coming back to these important tenets, and the upcoming chapters will illustrate how to use them in creating your BI program. In each future chapter, we will include helpful tips, case studies, and job aids. An electronic version of all the job aids will be available on the companion website.

CHAPTER 3

Data Quality

Everyone talks about data quality. Every vendor has a solution; every consultant offers a service that promises to address your data quality concerns. Bad data quality can impact everything that we strive for in business intelligence (BI). It can impact user adoption, perceived value, and the willingness of sponsors to support our efforts; it's the one thing that can kill a BI program. Data quality is important. Just like seatbelts are important. In other words, you don't necessarily have to invest in data quality (or wear a seatbelt) but there will likely come a day when you really wish you had and in that moment you will realize it's too late.

Good data quality drives value into the information that is provided to your business users. The commitment to treat your data as a corporate asset requires that you uniquely identify data and determine what "good" data looks like. Your businesspeople will know when they see bad data, and that will prevent them from making more informed decisions based on data. The focus for any data quality program should address the most common data issues, such as bad data entry or missing data.

Obviously I believe that data quality is important, but I would encourage a pragmatic focus on what is reasonable to accomplish. It's important to know that data quality has to be part of your BI effort before you start. First, we should all understand how data quality is defined. Perhaps the most famous definition is by Joseph Juran, a well-known management consultant and quality advocate: "Data are of high quality if they are fit for their intended uses in operations, decision making and planning." Another definition outlines the attributes of data quality:

Definition

Accuracy: The extent to which there are no errors.

Scope: The extent to which the breadth and depth of the data provide sufficient coverage of the event(s) of interest.

Timeliness: The extent to which data is received on time to take suitable actions and decisions.

Recency: The extent to which data is up to date relative to the event(s) of interest.

(Barua, 2011)

Simply put, data of high quality in your data warehouse should be error-free (no identification numbers with letters in them), include salient data points (such as diagnosis code for billing), and provide the data within hours or days (not weeks or months) to allow your business users to make decisions.

Data Quality Implications for Healthcare

The importance of good data quality cannot be underestimated; in a recent study on the value of data quality to organizations, it was found that even a 10 percent increase in the quality of data was attributable to $2 billion in revenue annually for a Fortune 1000 organization (Barua, 2011). That is money directly attributable to the improvement of usability of the data. So the importance of data quality is undeniable, but that doesn't mean that we drop everything and spend the next two years rebuilding the processes that create bad data. But it *does* mean that we control the quality of the data once it's in the data warehouse. You may have no control over the data before it gets to the data warehouse, but once it's there, you have complete control. That's an important distinction, and one that we want to remember as we move along. It doesn't mean that you shouldn't fix broken processes that create bad data (such as the inexplicable phenomenon of pharmacists leaning on the 9-key), but that's not always feasible and you don't want to get bogged down.

Data for healthcare organizations contained in the source systems is nearly useless. Many people wonder why data quality is so "bad" in healthcare, and whether it's worse than in other industries. The plain truth is that it is "bad" but bad is relative, and it is due to the transactional systems in healthcare. The transactional systems are meant to support the clinical workflow and not get in the way of providing care to the patient. For that reason, we don't require many fields, and often we don't require specific data types within fields. That means that data quality at the source, the transactional system where it's created, is poor.

It is a data quality best practice to fix the data at or as close to the source as you can get. That's not always feasible. We are not going back into a medical record and fix it, nor are we likely to ask care providers to interrupt their activities to ensure that they entered fields correctly. In some cases, that's critical, such as blood pressure (BP) where those fields should really be limited to three numbers, and not allow for letters, characters, or four or more numbers. But in most other cases we will make adjustments within the data warehouse. That doesn't mean that we will "fix" a BP recording if it is entered wrong, but we will become savvy about where data entry errors occur most often. Then we can rely on good data quality practices to determine where process changes must take place to ensure good data. When we see consistent inaccuracies of data based on process, that's referred to as "noisy" data and it can be very distracting. Extract, transform, and load (ETL) practices can address these noisy data and make them into information that's useful.

Another data quality issue is the nature of healthcare data. Healthcare data in its raw form has an enormous amount of detail, which represents itself in multiple rows. For the vast majority of users, the way we have data in its granular form, displaying each row of a record, is overkill. The fact that you have 217 rows of data for one encounter doesn't matter to most of your users. What does matter to them is the aggregated information associated with those 217 rows of data. This means that the ETL process becomes incredibly important. During ETL you pull these 217 rows of data into one record for the average end-user. To do that well, you have to apply the business rules for the data, and that is where data governance comes in. Business rules are the definitions and parameters for how the data needs to be transformed to be usable for a broader audience. Business rules cover everything from patient identifiers (must always be 8 digits) or birthdates (can't have a "13" in the month field, for example). In the beginning the idea that you will have a business rule for the majority of your data may sound overwhelming, but you won't tackle this task all at once.

As mentioned above, bad data quality can impact everything that we strive for in BI. But what is data quality, really? Do any of us have "clean" data? I can promise you that no one does. So what's the solution to improving data quality? Data governance.

Data Governance

No one wants more bureaucracy. That's why I endorse a small but focused approach to data governance. Organizations hesitate to implement data governance because they fear it will add an unnecessary level of red tape to BI projects. The truth is that it has many benefits. It improves user adoption and fosters the management of data as a corporate asset. Its primary function is to ensure an acceptable amount of data quality. By creating consistent definitions of data, it enables better decision making. Good data governance programs require collaboration among business units, and that collaboration drives an important aspect of data governance: the appropriate use of data. For healthcare, data governance is critical to regulatory compliance. A solid data governance function, with the appropriate amount of documentation, assists in meeting regulatory compliance and corresponding audits.

Definition: Data Governance

"Data Governance is a system of decision rights and accountabilities for information-related processes, executed according to agreed-upon models which describe who can take what actions with what information, and when, under what circumstances, using what methods."

(Thomas, 2004)

Strictly from a user-adoption perspective, creating a data governance function helps build trust in the process of delivering reports and analysis as well as the data itself. Tools don't solve data governance problems, process does. So in the beginning, avoid the inclination to purchase software that promises to help with data governance. The products may help, but they don't do the hard work of helping your organization define a patient, a stay, or a procedure.

The two primary layers of data governance are the governance committee and the data stewards. First, the committee is usually made up of leaders in your organization. As a matter of fact, it is best if you can get executives to sit on this committee, because then it will be easier to implement the changes to remedy bad data in your source systems. The second layer is the data stewards. They are integral to the long-term success of BI. These two layers will be my focus, as I give you small, achievable steps to get started or restarted in BI. Large, very complex data governance functions can often get in the way of getting started. I firmly believe that good data governance functions need to be dynamic and agile.

Tip

Check out the companion website (www.wiley.com/go/healthcarebi) for downloadable resources on data governance.

You will start by creating a governance committee, either by creating a brand new one or repurposing an existing group (see Figure 3.1). Your organization probably has a committee at an executive or senior level that meets regularly for either strategic or operational purposes. If you don't know offhand, do some research and find out who chairs the meeting. Ask the chair or their designee who is on the roster of participants, ask how frequently they meet and determine what their agenda usually covers. Ask if you can be put on the agenda and present to the committee the data governance imperative. You will want to make sure that you cover why data governance is so important, what it can bring to the organization, and how much time it will require of this committee, then ask the team to take on data governance. If this isn't possible, then you will have to create a new committee. In either case, make sure that your committee

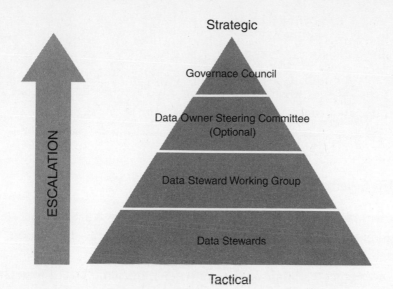

FIGURE 3.1 Data Governance Pyramid

has a representative from each functional area (financial, nursing, clinical, etc.). Anyone who is the guardian of data or has an interest in using data should participate. That number could get unwieldy in some organizations, which is why we go as high up the hierarchy as we can.

Your governance committee will be strategic in its function, and once it is up and running will make determinations on issues that get escalated to it. For example, if the data stewards cannot agree on a resolution for a data quality problem, or defining a broadly shared term such as "patient" or "member," the committee will decide.

Tip

Good data that is easily adopted allows your organization to transition from instinct-based decision making to data-based decision making, but that requires effort. Identify how long the commitment will be for the executives. The effort will be more intensive in the long run, so make sure that you position the advantages of their involvement up front, so they understand the payoff for their time.

Data Governance Organizational Charter

A sample structure for a data governance organization is provided below, with roles and responsibilities for each function.

Governance Committee: Executive/Senior Staff (Data Owners) Leading Business Units

- Creates policies and procedures associated with BI and data management
- Enforces policies and procedures
- Ensures that work of data management/IT/information management team is aligned with corporate strategy
- Champions BI and data governance to broader organization
- Reviews and approves recommendations from the data stewards regarding terms and definitions, quality standards, and thresholds

Data Steward: Subject Matter Expert Aligned with Business Units Represented on the Governance Committee

- Reviews issues with data and makes recommendations
- Ensures that work is aligned with policies and procedures
- Ensures proper usage, accessibility, and quality of the information within their data domain
- Establishes enterprise-wide standards for data quality and appropriate usage
- Ensures conformity, extensibility, security, and compliance

The first order of business for the governance committee is to identify your data stewards. Your governance committee should have representatives from each major administrative and clinical department and IT, and stewards should follow suit, although it's not critical to have a formal IT representative among the data stewards. Because IT is an important partner and enables your success, IT should serve as an advisor for both functions; however, they don't have voting rights.

Another preliminary task for your committee is to decide what your organization's acceptable level of data quality is. Certainly, 100 percent data quality sounds great, but there is no such thing. Personally, I have never seen 100 percent clean data. Healthcare data is entered by humans, so it is inherently flawed. You can create standards to improve quality, but you will never reach 100 percent. So your committee will have to decide what "good enough" quality is for your organization, and help everyone understand that data quality costs money. The cost difference between achieving 97 percent and 100 percent quality is huge, but the value you get from that additional 3 percent may not justify the expense. Get a data quality standard in place right away, or you risk getting "wrapped around the axle" in your other discussions about data.

Keep in mind that you can have a different threshold of acceptance for different data types. The best way to determine your data quality threshold is to assess the types of analysis and decisions you make with this data. For example, we know that finance data decisions keep money coming into the organization. Even a 5 percent aberration from reality can have a significant impact to the bottom line; therefore, finance data should have a high level of quality. The same goes for clinical data; if you are using this data for clinical research there is no room for error. That should imply, however, in both cases that you have a good amount of control over the source systems of this data. The methodical way to make this assessment is to ask three questions (see Table 3.1).

Now that you have formed a committee and decided what an acceptable level of data quality is, you can get started on the actual work of data governance. That work begins with the data stewards. Data stewards are the life-blood of your data governance function. The best data steward is someone who resides in your organization as a systems analyst or an applications analyst and is already the go-to person for questions about the data from the source system. Every company has these people—they tend to be very much in demand and tough for a department to relinquish. Many departments know it's the right thing to do, but it's a bit like giving up your morning coffee habit because you know it's better for you in the long run. In the beginning you feel tired and have a headache, but in a couple of weeks you won't miss it (coffee) or them (data stewards).

So how do you find a great data steward? First, write a job description. Many companies confuse the role of data owner or lead data steward with data steward, but they are distinct roles. Data owners are the people ultimately responsible for how the data is defined. They approve changes to metrics; they are advised by data stewards. Data owners are typically higher up in the organization (directors, for example). Anything that the data owners can't resolve gets resolved by the data governance committee. A lead data steward or chief data steward is responsible for ensuring that all the policies and procedures created by the data governance committee are carried out. In many cases, the lead or chief data steward writes the policies and procedures that are then ratified by the data governance committee. Many job descriptions for data stewards available today combine these roles into one, but this is a mistake. They are distinct roles that need to be supported by different people in your organization at different leadership and skill levels.

TABLE 3.1 Assessing High-Level Data Quality Standards

Question	Response	Comments	Examples
What types of decisions will you be making with this data?	1 - Mission critical 2 - Important 3 - Of interest	The lower the score the higher the data quality standard	Finance systems or clinical trials
How much control do you have over your source system?	1 - Excellent 2 - Very good 3 - Good 4 - Fair 5 - Poor	The better your control over the source system, the more likely you are to be able to maintain high-level data quality standards	Systems that you own, or where you have good control over the data entry
What is the cost of fixing the data?	1 - Low 2 - Medium 3 - High	Typically, the less control you have over your source system, the greater the odds that it will be expensive to "fix" the data	Low control means that you can't fix the data at the source, forcing you to manage complex ETL methods

Definition: Data Steward Job Description

The data steward's role is to strategically manage assigned data entities across the enterprise, while ensuring high levels of data quality, integrity, availability, and privacy. This individual is responsible for standardizing data naming, establishing consistent data definitions, and monitoring/auditing the data quality. The data steward should focus on business benefits, foster the goal of data reuse, and articulate the strategic significance of information to the organization. Other responsibilities include, but are not limited to:

- Serving as the single point of contact for an assigned data entity
- Maintaining and enhancing the overall quality of the data from each source system as part of a dedicated group of individuals
- Performing data quality checks for each data source system
- Resolving profile and affiliation issues on a case-by-case basis

Accountabilities:

- Work with the lead data steward to help uphold data governance policies and procedures to ensure standardized data naming, establish consistent data definitions, and monitor overall data quality for assigned data entities.
- Ensure that data management methodologies include the steps, activities, and deliverables required to consistently achieve high-quality data.
- Ensure that the systems adhere to defined data management practices, policies, and procedures. Identify and

manage the resolution of data quality issues, such as uniqueness, integrity, accuracy, consistency, and completeness in a cost-effective and timely fashion.

Job Requirements:

- BA/BS Accounting/Computer Science/Business/MIS (or equivalent work experience to substitute for education); master's a plus
- Strong understanding of relational database structures, theories, principles, and practices
- Experience with data processing flowcharting techniques preferred
- Demonstrated leadership skills
- Must be able to represent the data management team as a key subject matter expert and resource for the assigned data entity
- Exceptional analytical, conceptual, and problem-solving abilities
- Strong written, technical documentation and oral communication skills
- Strong presentation and interpersonal skills
- Ability to present ideas in user-friendly language
- Ability to prioritize and execute tasks in a high-pressure environment
- Experience working in a team-oriented, collaborative environment

Next you must decide how much time the data steward will dedicate to the task. This will help determine if you need to dedicate a full-time employee to fill the position or just need an employee to add this role to his or her existing responsibilities. This depends on the scope and nature of the work at hand.

Answering these four questions can help you determine what you need:

1. How many source systems hold data that you need to manage?
2. How many of those source systems are "key" to your business? In healthcare the EHR (electronic health record) or claims adjudication systems would be a key system.
3. Do you currently have any data quality procedures in place today?
4. Are you completing your BI (business intelligence)/DW (data warehouse) project in phases?

If you have a big number for Questions 1 and 2 and answered no to Questions 3 and 4, you need full-time data stewards. If you have a low number for Questions 1 and 2 and answered yes to 3 and 4, then you may be able to have an employee add this to his or her current responsibilities. However, it may still be best to have one full-time data steward for each of your key systems. Those systems will likely be involved in all the phases of your BI/DW projects.

After you have a job description and know the time commitment necessary, your next step is to make a presentation to your data governance committee. (If you do not have one, stop here and go back to the beginning of this chapter. No data steward will be successful without a governance committee directing his or her work.) Present a formal request to your governance committee to fill the data steward position(s). Your best data stewards are embedded in existing departments today. You have to convince the committee that giving them up to become data stewards is better for the company than leaving them where they are. Some key pieces of information to convey in this presentation are:

- These targeted employees are already doing work that could be defined as data stewardship.

- Data stewards will reside in the business, to stay close to the users of the source system.
- Good data quality can positively impact the bottom line of the company.
- Bad data quality can put the company at risk.
- Stewardship will improve our ability to make decisions based on data (not on hunches).
- Supporting appropriate use of data is important.

It's the responsibility of the governance committee to ensure that the organization's data is governed appropriately. That duty should encourage them to identify the data stewards for their departments. If a department can't name a steward, then human resources (HR) may have to start searching for one.

As you look for a data steward, remember that data and source systems can be taught, but the ability to communicate effectively to a broad audience, foster the goal of data reuse (data reuse provides consistency across the organization), and articulate the strategic significance of information to the organization cannot be taught. I recently had a conversation with a lead data steward and I asked him what the most important attribute of a data steward was. He said "communication." The ability to have a democratic approach and build trust and support was far more important to him than the knowledge of relational data structures, data modeling basics, or data analysis experience. All of these abilities are helpful, but the ability to communicate was the foremost attribute in the data stewards that he selected. Good communicators make good data stewards.

Another critical attribute is the ability to consider opposing viewpoints and come to a reasonable resolution. If you want to see your analysts get fired up, put them all in a room with a couple of data stewards and tell them you are changing the definition of a field. That is exactly what you should do, but it's a painful experience. The data steward's ability to manage those conversations is absolutely critical to the long-term success of the program.

When looking for a data steward, it's important to remember these things:

- Write a job description.
- Look at your existing staff to see who is already fulfilling this role.
- Rely on your governance committee.
- Seek out the good communicators.

Tip

The types of obstacles the governance function will face change as the organization matures and gets used to the idea of governance. In the beginning, no one will want to give up a person to be a data steward, but as the activity starts to bring value, departments will complain that they haven't been asked to participate. Prepare yourself for the changing obstacles over time.

Once you find your data stewards the next step is to outline the responsibilities of each of these governance layers. The senior staff is just kept informed for the most part, but they have absolute decision-making power. If you are unable to resolve an issue at a lower level, it has ultimate authority. The decision-making layer of governance should get quite engaged with settling data disputes, but its primary function is to set the policy and procedures for the governance function as a whole. Members should meet every other month to review the policies and procedures, to ensure compliance, and to resolve any concerns. These policies and procedures will help the newly

minted governance function operate. The policies and procedures document will:

- Document a mission statement for the governance function
- Outline roles and responsibilities for the governance func-
  tion
- Provide an organizational chart of data governance
- Determine minimum levels of participation
- Document escalation procedures
- Determine decision factors for high-level data standards
- Establish decision rights of each governance layer

Tip: Check Out Our Companion Website

A downloadable policies and procedures template can be
found on the companion website (www.wiley.com/go/
healthcarebi).

Getting Started with Data Governance

First, the team will need to decide where to begin. Do not attempt to boil the ocean. Data governance programs can quickly
get overwhelmed by the sheer volume of data that needs to be
harnessed and defined. If you are starting a BI project, just begin with the data points that are associated with a subject area
(e.g., claims). If you have a BI program in place but are attempting to get data governance up and running, then perhaps it's
best to start with the key metrics your organization uses, such
as revenue cycle metrics, or cost and utilization. Either way,
the important thing is to get started with a small, achievable
set of metrics. For this first phase, meeting every other week is
reasonable. After that, the team can meet on an as-needed basis.

The easiest way to do this is to create a queue of report
requests. This is easy because most end-users think in terms of

reports, not necessarily analysis or even metrics. If you have been doing any type of reporting then you probably have a backlog of requests. To prepare for apples-to-apples comparisons it is best to ask a consistent set of questions. These questions will allow you to consider each request on two scales: business value and ease of implementation. Business value allows you to assess the impact the report will provide to the business. These questions should be about customer requests, regulatory needs, or new service or product lines. The ease of implementation questions should explore the level of complexity to create the new report from a technical perspective. These questions should ask whether the data is currently available or requires a new data source; it should also ask if the report exists in a reasonable form through another avenue (such as a team of analysts).

Tip: Check Out Our Companion Website

A downloadable sample survey is available in the companion website (www.wiley.com/go/healthcarebi).

For each request you will map it to a quadrant (see Figure 3.2). On the y axis is the business value scale; on the x axis is the ease of implementation scale. The logic is fairly simple: Anything that is easy to do and has high business value should get the green light (the upper left quadrant). Requests with low business value that are complex will be in the lower right quadrant. These are typically the requests that you can't complete because you don't have an enterprise data warehouse, and they make great ammunition for the case to build a data warehouse. The remaining requests in the upper right and lower left quadrants should be prioritized by your governance committee.

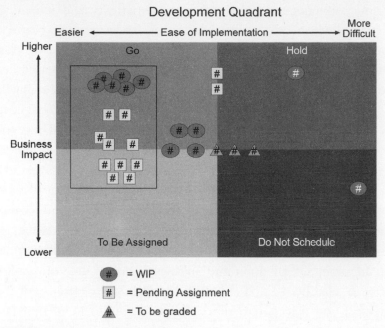

FIGURE 3.2 Development Quadrant

This queue becomes your data quality list. You will need to assign data stewards to each project to ensure that the data quality standards are met for each metric in the report. This will allow you to continue to deliver value to end-users and also to create a set of "certified" data.

Definition: Certified Data

The concept of data certification simply means that the data that is released, whether in a report or through an ad hoc analysis, meets the level for data quality that your data governance committee has set. This formal method of data certification includes identification that the data is certified (such as the footer in a report, or an announcement on the log-on screen of the business intelligence application).

As you move through the queue, the participation of the data stewards will become less and less necessary because you will have already certified the data. As you add new data to your warehouse, a data steward will need to create the definitions and acceptable parameters for the new data.

For a data warehouse project where all the data is new, you should assign data stewards to the subject areas. Then you complete the certification of data iteratively, as you bring on new subject areas. Deciding which subject areas to do first can be done through a process similar to the prioritization of your queue. But, rather than dealing with business value and ease of implementation, you can assess how frequently the data will be used. Those data points that are most frequently used or relied on in other calculations and metrics become the foundation of your warehouse and should be built first. Regardless of the method you select, remember that you should keep the data certification process to smaller achievable sets of data; otherwise the exercise gets too overwhelming.

Data Profiling

In our pursuit of high-quality data, data profiling is a powerful tool. Although it sounds like a technical exercise, in reality it is much more an analytic exercise. It is our effort to lay claim to the data as it exists directly from the source systems.

In an academic setting the concept of analyzing data that already exists is generally referred to as applied research. The goal of business intelligence is to use this "applied" data to find the nuggets of gold that will transform your organization. My passion, education, and experience all revolve around applied data, but it is full of challenges. The most significant challenge is that you are strapped to that data, attached for good or bad. You will have to rely on the data, but to find the nuggets you have to understand what the data has to offer. We call this data profiling.

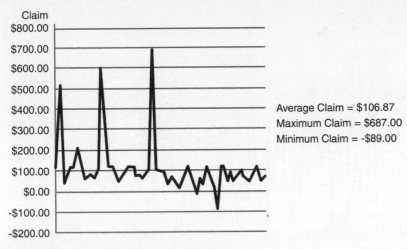

FIGURE 3.3 Claims Data Quality Analysis

This concept of data profiling allows you to understand the data at a detail level; specifically, you will ascertain how error-prone the data is. You can use everyday tools to do this work, such as Microsoft Excel. Excel allows you to run descriptive statistics on the data, and that is what you are looking for. Those descriptive statistics, the mean, median, mode, range, minimum, and maximum, will provide a clear picture of how well the data behaves (see Figures 3.3 and 3.4).

The gap is the important piece—the gap between what the data is and what you want the data to be. As your data governance committee determines what the data *should* look like, and you determine what the data *does* look like, you will have to come up with a plan to close the gap. Once you close the gap and load the data into the data warehouse, you can then certify it for usage. Closing the gap requires ETL capabilities. We discuss ETL a great deal in Chapter 5. For data profiling purposes, all we need to know about ETL is that the scripts that are written to load the data must apply the business rules that will make that data useful. Although the data stewards may assist

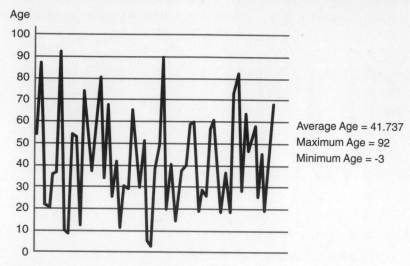

FIGURE 3.4 Age Data Quality Analysis

in some of the data definitions and business rules creation, that exercise can be done as part of a business requirements effort for each new report, dashboard, or data subject area.

For example, perhaps we have a business rule that says that our unique patient identifier is nine digits long. As we profile our data we find that 2 percent of the data is 10 digits long; we also find that there are instances where the unique identifier isn't unique (i.e., it's attributed to more than one individual). Let's also say that our data governance committee has decided that every one of our records should have a unique patient identifier, which means that we have to fix our errors. The ETL script that is written will purposefully throw out a patient ID that is longer than nine digits or contains characters into a log file. That log file should be reviewed frequently, and the review will likely reveal a process breakdown that will require process changes. The governance committee should review a "highlight reel" of the log file, as it will most likely impact their teams the most from a process modification perspective.

Data profiling is a slippery slope. If you unleash a team of analysts on the data, they will likely never be happy with what they discover about the data. An analyst's perspective of data is different from everyone else's. Therefore, you have to select specific data or a subject area to analyze, and you will have to time-box the activity for the analysts.

The time-box serves an important function. It prevents the potential of analysis paralysis by identifying the specific amount of time that you are willing to invest in this activity. Depending on the volume of data, this activity could be limited to one week. The important thing is that you gain as much information as possible in the shortest time possible.

The activity should be straightforward, and for this type of analysis you don't need your rock-star analysts to get distracted. Because the statistics that you need on the data are basic (mean, median, mode, etc.) you can have a new analyst or even a data-savvy businessperson lead the charge. There are some excellent products available that make spotting errant data incredibly easy (see Figure 3.5). In the picture below the product uses MP3

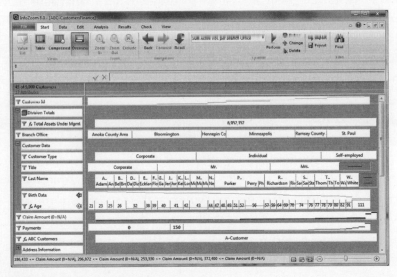

FIGURE 3.5 Data Profiling Screen Shot

compression technology to be able to graph a large amount of data so that any end-user can quickly ascertain where the outliers are, and drill down from there. These powerful tools help organizations quickly assess their data quality.

Tip: Check Out Our Companion Website

To learn more about data profiling products, visit the companion website (www.wiley.com/go/healthcarebi).

Data Governance: Step by Step

You will need:

- To identify a project that will bring the organization value
- To identify an existing committee that can be repurposed as your executive committee or create a new committee
- A data steward
- A queue of requests
- A data governance policies and procedures template

Directions:

Take a quick inventory of the things that are in your queue of requests to determine if there are any projects that would be of value to the organization as the pilot BI effort. It's important to keep value at the top of your mind. Approach the executive committee that you would like to repurpose and make your case. Be sure to have done your research. Chapter 4 on leadership and sponsorship will talk more about how to best present your case to this group. For now, just know that the group will care about the value this brings to the organization.

Assuming that you are able to gain the support of the executive committee members you will need to have them identify the data stewards for the subject areas that you are going to tackle. This may take a couple of iterations with the committee. You will have to schedule one-on-one meetings to explain the data steward role and why someone should give you a resource to this project—this will require some patience.

Once the data stewards have been identified you will need to complete the policies and procedures document that will outline how your data governance function will operate. The template for this is available in the companion website, and a reference to it is in the back of this book. The basics of this document are:

- The value of data governance
- Mission statement
- Governance structure
- Minimum expectations for participation
- Roles and responsibilities
- Escalation procedures
- Roster
- High-level data standards
- Data governance decision rights
- Glossary

The completion of the policies and procedures guide will help you introduce the new function to the organization. You will know the "who, what, and how" of the governance function.

You should have a data governance committee, a couple of data stewards identified, a project to focus on, and the completed policies and procedures document. Next, you will have to determine the level of data quality associated with the data that you will be using for your project.

Identify the data that you need and time-box the data-profiling exercise. At this point we won't be tackling the errant data, we just need to know how big the gap is between what we have in our source systems and what we need in the data warehouse to consider our data to be "certified for usage."

Tip

Create a method to promote that your data is certified. Put a statement in the footer of your reports, or a gold seal on the log-in page of your BI application. Either way, make sure users know the lengths you go to ensure highly usable data.

Case Study: Data Quality Is King

Blue Health Intelligence (BHI) is the nation's premiere health intelligence resource, delivering data-driven insights about healthcare trends, care effectiveness, and best practices. BHI accesses healthcare claims data from more than 110 million lives nationwide in a safe and secure database. The resulting reliable, conformed data set has the broadest, deepest pool of integrated medical and pharmacy claims in the country, reflecting healthcare services delivered in every ZIP code.

Today, BHI accesses the largest database of its kind. But more important than its size, BHI has an ability to provide a high degree of value to the healthcare industry as a whole. As the BHI project began, and throughout its history, the creators and stewards of this database focused on high-quality data. They recognized early on that the value of the analytics would suffer without it. Andrea Marks, chief informatics officer of BHI, puts it in these terms: "Once data goes awry your interpretation of the output goes awry and that becomes exponential. You have to put the focus on the data. Data is king; it's got to be of high quality."

Data used for BHI analytics undergoes four levels of certification, including an independent external actuarial review, which "ensures we have the strongest foundation possible," says Swati Abbott, chief executive officer, BHI. As a result, BHI builds predictive models in unparalleled ways, supporting care management, identifying at-risk patients, and determining appropriate levels of care and effective disease management programs. BHI's predictive analytics capabilities can even identify patient risk factors for rare conditions that have eluded other organizations, allowing clients to proactively address those factors.

Predictive modeling will be increasingly used to determine at-risk patients. "Without a foundation built from reliable, conformed data, we would not be able to utilize robust analytic capabilities to deliver actionable insights to our clients," says Abbott. For example, it is estimated that half of all Americans will have diabetes or pre-diabetes by 2020, which will account for more than 10 percent of healthcare spending. Abbott states, "Our clients want to be able to identify who is at risk and how they can proactively mitigate those risks." BHI analytics provides insights that can help healthcare providers improve quality of care, reduce overall patient health risks, and advance patient care.

Although its impressive data and database capabilities have undoubtedly been key to BHI's success, Marks emphasizes quality over all else when building a data set. "Without quality data," she says, "users won't trust the outcomes. There has to be a laser focus on the quality of data that you're adding to your database. Without the ability to effectively capture and utilize high-quality data, the analytical power of the data is compromised and your outputs could be adversely affected." Her guidance is simple and pragmatic. "Start small, utilizing an iterative approach, and focus on adding value to your organization." She continues, "Data is core to the business—it's no longer just the CFO interested in numbers. The data, though complex, can be structured in a way to make it both effective and useful."*

---

*Blue Health Intelligence is an independent licensee of the Blue Cross and Blue Shield Association. Blue Health Intelligence (BHI) is a trade name of Health Intelligence Company, LLC.

Notes

Barua, A. M. (2011). *Measuring the Business Impacts of Effective Data*. Austin: University of Texas, Austin.

Thomas, G. (2004). "Data Governance Definitions." Data Governance Institute. Retrieved March 9, 2012, from http://www.datagovernance.com/adg_data_governance_definition.html.

CHAPTER 4

Leadership and Sponsorship

As you read the case studies throughout this book, the one thing you will notice consistently is the strong voice of a leader. Sometimes the leader is someone new to the organization, but usually it is a person who has been there for a while. Either way, the voice of this leader has left an indelible mark on the business intelligence (BI) program. He or she has, through sheer force of will, a passion for the "rightness" of the program, conquered new territory to create a program that transformed the organization. All of us can learn a lot from these leaders; sometimes these lessons are obvious, such as a focus on data quality, while others aren't as obvious.

Each time I go to a new organization I look for certain characteristics that will spell trouble for the BI initiative. As a consultant, that helps me determine where I might run into trouble down the road. Being an objective third party makes it much easier to spot the red flags. I look for things like support from the IT group, focus on data quality, organizational structures, and strong data models, but I focus much of my attention on determining the leader and sponsor of the BI initiative. Sometimes that's the same person, but often it isn't. Just because you have a sponsor doesn't mean that your program is completely set for success. Success requires much more than leadership and sponsorship, which is why the other tenets exist.

But strong leadership and sponsorship can help create the right foundation to address the other tenets.

I read a Twitter feed a while back that postulated the only reason that BI programs need executive sponsorship is so consultants can have someone to sell to. Well, I disagree with that tweet. What I found over the years is that without a strong executive sponsor, I wasn't able to gain traction—and that was when I was a BI director, not a consultant. The way that I define sponsorship for BI programs requires multiple participants, active participation, and a level of knowledge that makes any sponsor an active member of the BI team.

Sponsorship and leadership can be two different things, so we will discuss them separately. For the purposes of this book, leadership is defined as the individual who will be accountable for the successful execution of the BI program. Sponsors support the activity by evangelizing it throughout the organization, providing financial support and serving in the governance function. Some leadership and sponsorship activities will overlap; for example, leaders will evangelize as well. First we will discuss leadership of a BI program. I am a strong advocate for servant leadership, so you will see that preference. Leadership is a critical component to sponsorship, which we will discuss in detail.

Leading a BI Initiative

Leadership is a difficult thing. For some it comes naturally, but even for those people the role of leader has its challenges. BI as a function has to serve many masters in an organization. When done well, BI is delivering value to the entire organization, which means that you have to balance the needs of one department or team against another. Part of the BI journey is to define and manage data, which often leads to challenging conversations around ownership and process improvements. Data quickly highlights where your weak processes are.

BI leaders must have a strong passion for what BI can deliver to the organization and a willingness to let go so it can become something greater than one person. They also need an ability to doggedly persevere through countless obstacles. When I talk to BI leaders in healthcare across the country, what I hear is enthusiasm. They express some frustrations, but these leaders know and understand what the value is and they continue in spite of these challenges.

As you consider or come to terms with your leadership of a BI program, here are some considerations:

- Make sure that you leave time for strategy.
- Get the right people in the right roles within your organization.
- Grow some thick skin—this isn't a popularity contest.
- When possible, build consensus, but know when to step in and keep things moving.

Strategy

Winston Churchill famously said, "He who fails to plan is planning to fail." I don't suppose that we all happily go into work in the morning planning on failing, but with BI initiatives it seems that is exactly what we do. Nine times out of 10 the BI programs that I see have virtually no plan for the next three months. They address the issues that come up day by day and deliver reports as requests come in. That will keep you busy, but it won't keep you safe. Part of the leadership of a BI program is to plan a longer-term vision for what BI can deliver to the organization. The true value of BI is more than just a set of reports, but a sustaining capability that provides your organization with insight. Anyone can manage it as an order-taking team, with only incremental value provided.

It is well advised to plan out the BI activities over a longer period of time. That requires some strategic planning, and one method is to use road maps for longer-term initiatives. For healthcare BI, these road maps are usually no longer than 18 months but should be no shorter than 12 months. As an activity they usually take about 12 to 14 weeks. You need to straddle the difference between strategic planning and project planning. Having a strategic vision and an 18-month road map will not only help guide your team but will also help your budget forecasting. The challenge with doing BI work without a plan is that you often don't realize that the decisions you are making have a downstream impact until you are, well, downstream.

Road-mapping exercises are strenuous. Contrary to the name "road map," which implies a nicely folded individual piece of paper, every road map I have written has been more than 50 pages. I wish it had been named a navigation panel. Road maps are static; navigation panels are dynamic, helping you avoid traffic delays and road construction. If you build your road map with the idea of being dynamic, and you have a schedule for revisiting your plan, you will be much better off. The key things to remember: (1) you need to know what your company needs, and (2) in what priority order. Your prioritization should come from both the business need (preferably weighted) and the technical complexity to implement. Once you know these two pieces of information you will be able to schedule content releases. Remember that as you complete your road map you will need to show business value quickly and often, otherwise you risk losing sponsorship.

The first time you do a strategic plan or road map you will have to invest more time in the following process:

1. Create a working group.
2. Determine list of interviewees.
3. Create interview questions.

4. Schedule interviews.
5. Complete interviews.
6. Analyze data from interviews.
7. Create categories of work.
8. Visualize analysis in road map view.
9. Present to BI governance council.
10. Present to organization.

You will need a group of people who can help you do the work for the road map. This group is different from the BI governance council, as these are the folks who will do the interviews, collect results, analyze results, and present the options to the council. Ideally, this will include the leader of the BI group, a business analyst, and an IT resource. The important thing to note for this work is that you are not solution-ing; you are just brainstorming ideas and understanding the needs of the business.

Your interview list should ideally include the business folks who have a fair amount of experience and can give you both a perspective on what they need (i.e., a dashboard) and the level of work that is required to get to the data today. This is usually a high-level manager who has an understanding of strategy, but has a good knowledge of what it would take from their team to get the job done. You also want to make sure that you cover all of the functional areas of your organization; leaving someone out might mean that they are not considered as part of the initial build for the BI program.

During these interviews, make sure that you get as much quantifiable information as possible: the number of hours it takes to run reports, validate data, any dollar figures associated with poor data quality, and so forth. That will help you build out your strategic assessment. During these interviews you should also be gaining insight into what your company would need from a BI program. When your interviews are done, you will

FIGURE 4.1 Road Map: Strategy to Execution

ideally have lots of fodder for your cost benefit analysis (CBA) or return on investment (ROI), and you will have plenty of requested business value from the interviews you conducted that will help you build out your road map (see Figure 4.1).

The next step in the process is relatively simple although very powerful when done correctly. First, you will want to define your business opportunity. A business opportunity is defined by the executives in your organization. These business opportunities are high level and help define what is valuable that the BI program can deliver. You should ask the question: What will this solve for you? Better reporting/analytics for customers? Competitive differentiator? Improved full-time equivalent (FTE) efficiency?

Once that is done, you will need to define the value associated with the opportunity. In other words, if we solve this, what does it provide? If we are able to solve for "better reporting and analytics" what does that do for the organization? These questions are critical to answer from a business perspective because it will help validate the solution later.

Next, you will need to identify the business case. A business case is one that currently exists or needs to exist to support the business value. In other words, if you are improving the reporting and analysis for clients, you will want to document every existing report and the associated logic with those reports, as well as any reports that were identified but don't exist yet. This is an important step because it gives you a sense of volume.

Once you have defined all the business cases, you have to break them down into consumable business requirements. If a developer were to pick up these documents, they should be able to deliver the solution.

Finally, you will need to determine what data is needed based on these requirements, and what data domains are impacted. These are the data points that will impact the solution. This will help you determine how technically difficult the implementation will be.

Once you have completed all that work, you need to score each item. The score is based on the technical complexity and the business value. Each of these scores should be taken as an entire business request from the business opportunity down to the data. The best way to do this is to use Excel and break each category apart. The scoring needs to occur at the most detailed level but it can (and should) be aggregated to the business request to deliver the high-level road map.

Tip: Check Out Our Companion Website

The website (www.wiley.com/go/healthcarebi) has a downloable template of the road map and the scoring sheet.

Once the first road map is done, it's recommended that you plan a little. If you only plan to be strategic once a year for the road map review, you may miss something. Put a little strategic planning into your regular schedule—that way, when review time comes up, it won't require so much focus.

The Right People in the Right Roles

We will discuss how to build your BI team in Chapter 6. For the purposes of this chapter, we explore team development and leadership. When you build the BI team and get the right leaders in the right role, you can do more. You'll also need to get comfortable with delegating; part of being a leader is to know when someone else can do the job. Keep in mind, though, that not all teams are created equal. It's common for changes in the organization to result in some significant disruption among team members. That includes new leadership being named, reorganizations, and so on. Remember that teams can frequently go through the "forming, storming, norming and performing" cycle (as defined by Bruce Tuckman in 1965 [Tuckman, 1965]). Your team will function better if you keep this in mind and strive to move through the stages as quickly as possible.

When leading a team, particularly a BI team, I have found it valuable to deconstruct the team members' motivations. I'm not advising an in-depth psychological analysis, but if you understand what motivates them, and how they learn, you can frame your conversations so they are in the best position to deliver. Many BI people are recovering IT professionals, and IT and data professionals are a different breed. An excellent book on this topic is *Leading Geeks*, which discusses the motivations of "geeks" and how to lead them (Paul Glen and David H. Maister, 2002).

Grow Thick Skin

I am not here to offer advice on how to be a better leader. What is important to me is to paint a clear picture of what it's like to lead a BI program. I have my theories as to why BI tends to attract the naysayers. My best guess is that it's because BI is very visible in most organizations. It usually has a number of people actively involved and when done well, that exposure can lead to good buy-in, support, and value. As a side effect, though, it often leads to criticism.

I remember a particularly stinging bit of criticism I received from an individual whom I respected a great deal. It was immediately following a series of focus group sessions with my user group. The group members were upset because we had a bad release. The meetings were tough enough to take, but I tried to stay positive because we were on the right path. The member sat down next to me after a particularly brutal session and said, "I don't think you've ever done this before. This meeting was terrible; I am going to escalate this to management." I was shocked. The feedback we received was tough to hear, but we owned the bad release. I didn't think that it called for any escalation; it was being managed quite well considering the circumstances.

I don't think it would have stung as much if I didn't like and respect this individual so much. Unfortunately, that was the beginning of the end for our good working relationship. I immediately became distrustful of his intentions and harbored some ill will for his (in my opinion) premature escalation of a relatively minor issue. I did, however, learn a lot from this situation, and I received some good guidance from my manager. The truth is, criticism is rampant in our society. I am not referring to the constructive kind that can help us all grow. I am talking about the kind of criticism that exists for less noble reasons. The worst part about criticism is that it is easier to believe than the positive stuff that happens; that's human nature. At one point or another, someone will come out swinging. Just know when to duck.

The Buck Stops with You

In my opinion, the best BI departments act as facilitators not owners. I use the analogy of government frequently: If I am letting my constituents down, I'm not doing my job. BI should be the bridge that brings the organization together. This requires a lot of heavy lifting to build the consensus that runs the BI program.

But it's not always possible to build consensus. I remember talking with someone on this topic and he asked me how I manage to build consensus but am able to abandon it when it's not working. I don't have a magic formula for this. I cannot tell you the exact phrase you'll hear that clearly indicates when consensus-building isn't working, but what I can tell you is that there will be a time. And when that time comes, you can't hesitate to step in and make a decision. The program must move forward, and you have to step up and be "the buck stops here" leader to maintain momentum. The lack of a decision introduces much more risk than the "wrong" decision.

This breakdown of consensus happens frequently in healthcare organizations. I think that our "decision-making-by-committee" in healthcare is the reason why BI hasn't been widely adopted. I have seen this firsthand, especially with hospitals. Consensus-building is an important part of the culture in hospital management. I am generalizing, but what I see too often is that different-minded, data-driven individuals all get together, call themselves some type of steering committee, and attempt to guide the BI program. They do not have one "leader," but rather a chair of the committee. If the committee is high performing and has decision rights articulated, you may be able to function this way, but I have often seen this approach wither and die.

Committees have their place. They are critical to guiding the business perspective of the BI program. They bring validation and buy-in to the broader audience. They should not, however, be the solution to every problem. Committees should be a part of the BI leadership, but there should also be a person who is ready to make decisions when the group gets stuck in indecision.

Case Study: A Leader Like This

I attended a chapter presentation of the Data Warehousing Institute (TDWI) in Minneapolis in 2011. The presenter was a friend of mine; we met a number of years ago as I was searching for someone who had led an organization through the data governance obstacle course. Darren Taylor is vice president at Blue Cross and Blue Shield of Kansas City. Darren has been there for more than 19 years now and has held many titles, but his current focus on BI, analytics, and data management has brought him and the organization national acclaim.

As Darren was wrapping up his presentation he answered a question from an audience member about how this work is really done. He answered that much of the work is organizational, cultural, and people-focused. The session ended and people stood around talking as usual. One person finally said, "You know, it's true what he said about it being organizational, cultural, and people-based, but that would be a lot easier with a leader like Darren."

If you ask Darren that question, "Do you think it's you?" as I did, he'll answer in a way that helps you understand his level of success. His answer will be something like "Well, that's very flattering, but I had good sponsorship and a whole team of really smart people ready to take on the challenge." I don't doubt that to be true, but how you keep smart people motivated and executives supportive has a lot to do with how the program is led. That's why that audience member wanted a leader like Darren.

To be clear, Darren has led his organization to do things that many organizations wished they could do with their data. They have an enterprise data warehouse that won a best practices award from TDWI (1105 Media, 2011), boasting a 332-percent return on investment, they have a fully functioning data governance program, and in 2010 Darren took on the challenge of creating an analytically focused BI program that is pushing the organization to new heights.

Darren has seen sponsorship change over time. In the beginning he had little sponsorship, but a change in leadership breathed new air into the sponsorship of the data management program and allowed Darren and his team to plan their future. Executing on that future requires leadership and sponsorship, something Blue Cross and Blue Shield of Kansas City has in spades.

Leadership Opportunities: The JAD Session

You have many opportunities as a leader to impact your program—so many, in fact, that I couldn't list them all if I tried. One opportunity that I will mention specifically is a JAD session, or joint application design. JAD sessions have been around for a long time in the IT industry. JAD sessions were created to allow for a project team to get into a room and have a facilitated discussion about what it wants the application to do. Many people have adapted JAD sessions for BI, and I think that's an excellent use of this methodology.

A few weeks ago I received a call from a friend of mine. He had recently taken on a new job and within his first 30 days, he isolated a project that had been stalled because they couldn't solidify the ad hoc requirements. They had been down the path for a number of months, and despite a number of good tries, the requirements continued to elude them. He knew that the best (and quickest) way to get over this hump was to complete a JAD session.

Tip: Check Out Our Companion Website

To learn more about JAD sessions, and how to run one for your program, go to our companion website (www.wiley .com/go/healthcarebi) for instructions and references.

Requirements can be a tricky business. Wrong requirements are blamed for many things, and they certainly present a major challenge for leaders of BI programs. JAD sessions, when run well, can really get at the heart of the requirements for anything: ad hoc environments, reports, dashboards, and so on. I run JAD sessions frequently to help my clients get their arms around their needs. In today's brave new world of increasing data volumes, we all assume that more is better, but it's not—at least not when it comes to data. Storing megabytes of click-stream data provides no tangible value to the average healthcare organization. JAD sessions, or any other method you use to get to the business requirements, should first focus on the business need and business value. Just because you *can* do something doesn't always mean you *should*.

As a leader, it's a good idea to invest in requirements. Find methods (such as JAD sessions) that work for your organization. Hire a business analyst with a good track record of getting to the core of the business request. As long as you make sure that the requirements represent business need and business value, you should do whatever you can to build them out. Prioritizing value is something we discussed in Chapter 3, and can be applied to any request to ensure that you are building the most valuable deliverable first (whether an ad hoc environment, a report, or a dashboard).

Why Sponsorship Is Critical

Sponsorship implies support. Different from leadership, sponsorship can be done by anyone in the organization. It's ideal to have sponsors who are leaders (to ensure the long-term success of your program), but leaders shouldn't be your only sponsors. You will need to have sponsors from all levels. Organizations change, people move around, others leave—but if you have support at each level of the organization, that's your protection against the inevitable staff changes.

I have seen the value of good leadership and sponsorship for a BI program. During my first few months at one organization, my boss asked me to "do that BI thing." I had taken a position there as an analyst, hoping to get off the BI consultant train (i.e., airplane). I agreed, because (beside the fact that he was my boss) I really felt that BI could be beneficial to the organization.

Then I realized I had to tackle the hard part. No one at the organization knew what BI really was. They thought they had a "data warehouse," had invested in tools, and even had something that looked like a process—so what could they possibly need? The leadership of the organization felt that the "Decision Support" department was just a group of complainers who couldn't deliver. That was far from the truth, but it was their perception. The truth was that they had purchased a data model that was a complete black box on outdated technology and the group of "complainers" were some very talented resources who were doing incredible things with really bad technology. We were in trouble. The discrepancy between perception and reality was so large I couldn't even see the other side. The leadership was less than inclined to financially support complainers, but without a budget I couldn't really impact change.

I had to do two things to keep from getting fired: (1) create a team that was more effective; and (2) ensure that people had easier access to the information they needed for their jobs. Without support, and therefore no budget, that wasn't an easy task. The first thing I did was create a "Reporting Task Force." I couldn't really call it BI yet, because there wasn't much BI going on. What was going on, however, was a complete misperception about what was happening. My goal was to create the right kind of transparency. The team thought they were telling the end-users why things weren't getting worked on, but in reality the end-users only heard a litany of excuses. It was really about spin control. I told my boss it was like walking past a house with no curtains: everyone could see into our messy, disorganized house. If we were going to continue without curtains, we needed to ensure that our house was in order.

We created a queue of all the outstanding requests. From that queue we created a standard method of scoring each of them. Chapter 3 discusses this in depth, but for the purposes of executive sponsorship it's important to understand that we had to get our house in order by creating repeatable processes, consistent communication, and understandable explanations—all in the name of reasonable expectations.

Once that was underway, I knew I needed to seek out my sponsors. I felt strongly that I needed to have more than one, and in "SponsorLand," not all sponsors are created equal.

In Search of a Sponsor

Sponsors don't sign up to support BI programs without a good reason. Whether they determine the value as a result of a conversation inside the organization, or have heard other organizations do great things with BI, one way or another they have to understand the value that BI can bring to everyone. What we seek for sponsorship are high-quality sponsors who want to deliver a good product to the entire organization. I have seen situations where the executive sponsor uses the project as his personal work team and requires prioritization of only his projects. That's not good sponsorship. You will need to balance the sponsor's needs against everyone else's, and it's important that your sponsor understand that.

I knew I had to find an executive who had the most to lose without good reports. I needed to find someone with a sincere need and a willing attitude. Sincerity is probably the operative word here; it doesn't mean that they have management objectives that are tied to success of the program. It means that they can't do their job without data informing their decision making. Have the sponsor share his or her current perceptions, then carefully reveal the current reality.

My first conversation with my selected executive sponsor was about risk: the risk of data exposure and the risk of "bad" data to clients. I didn't get into details; I just told him that we were at an increased risk of inadvertent personal health information (PHI) disclosures. We were also at risk for sharing data with clients that could be interpreted as "wrong." I planted the seed and walked away. I set up a meeting a few days later to get into the details. Up until this point, no one had sat down with him to explain in his words what the issues were. Prior to this, he had only heard explanations that included query logic and terms like "referential integrity." His past reaction was always "Fix it!" because he didn't understand the impact. Once he was engaged in understanding the problem and the risks, I could begin explaining how we got there. It is important that you speak in plain terms to keep your executive sponsors informed—not IT speak.

After projecting a strong ROI for the project, I received some incremental support to switch out technology. Once that was complete, we started talking about more complicated aspects of BI programs. Eventually, that senior VP could stand toe-to-toe with the CIO and defend the program, protecting and supporting it to make it the key differentiator that it is today.

What Is an "Executive Sponsor"?

Just to be clear, this **isn't** a checkbox activity. Just having a sponsor isn't enough. Look for someone who has a lot to lose without BI. You need a sponsor who is highly engaged in the project and will always be an advocate for your program when the boardroom door closes. To maintain this support, you must keep your sponsor in the loop. You must be the one to personally educate your sponsor and keep them up to speed. Allowing anyone else to do it creates a risk that the program's success will be defined by someone else's standards.

Let's review the two approaches you can take regarding sponsorship. The first is the "ask forgiveness, not permission" approach. Here, you try to build something to win over the executives and then build something that will demonstrate the value of BI—and as a result, you gain executive sponsorship (for the larger investment). The advantage to this approach is speed. The disadvantage is that if you do build something that is useful, the executives may question the need for investment if you are able to pull it off for next to nothing. The risk you take is really up to you.

The second approach is the old-fashioned way—gaining sponsorship in advance. If you are like me and feel that BI programs are not the time to stick your neck out, then gaining a sponsor first is preferable. With either approach, you will eventually need a sponsor for the financial aspect of support.

Your executive sponsor is critical because you can't be in the boardroom every time your project comes up, and if it's expensive it will come up often. So make sure that your sponsor is well informed and highly engaged. It could mean the difference between funding and ending.

Types of Sponsors

It may come as a surprise to you, but there are many different types of sponsors. Each of the sponsors has his or her unique perspective and provides you with a level of support that will be valuable to the BI organization in the long run. They also each come with their own set of organizational "baggage" and will require some level of attention to ensure their participation (see Figure 4.2).

Ideally, at least one of your sponsors is as high up in the organization as possible. This type of sponsor is the traditional executive sponsor, such as someone in the "C" suite or a (senior) vice president. Every organization is a bit different in what it considers its senior staff, so the person we are looking for has

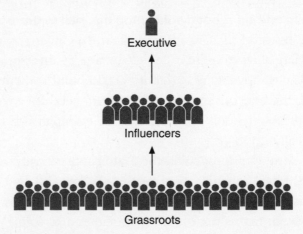

FIGURE 4.2 Types of Sponsors

a formal leadership position and therefore has the authority to remove obstacles to the program. The challenge is that the person in this role is hard to access, and is short on time. If you are able to get a meeting, be concise and efficient. Make sure that you have your case well documented and rehearsed. Be prepared for the conversation to go in alternate directions (such as, "What are the next steps?" or "What do you think we should do?" or "What's the financial investment?").

Be prepared to discuss things like return on investment, and if possible refer him or her to another program that has been successful (references such as the TDWI Best Practice Awards are excellent). Try to do some research in advance on your chosen executive. Talk to other people and find out the hot buttons that will be persuasive. Maybe it's risk management or compliance to federal mandates. Maybe they get really frustrated by not having easy access to answers, or getting multiple answers to the same question. Make sure that whatever their hot button is, you have a well-coordinated answer to address it.

A second type of sponsor is called the *Influencer*. Influencers are the people who may not have the "right" title (such as CFO) but are well trusted by those in the organization who do have the right titles. It's likely to be easier to get a meeting with these people, but they will want to know the same things that people in the targeted role would. Specifically, they are going to want to know why they should stick their neck out (and spend their political clout) to champion this project, so you have to be prepared to answer the question "What's in it for me?"

What's in it for these sponsors is affiliation with a project that could be a giant win for your organization. You have to sell all of the possibilities to them, and get them excited about where this BI program could take your organization. Even better, take some of the success stories from this book and apply them to

85

your organization. What if we did this? What would happen? The more specific you can be about the benefits, the easier it will be for them to support the project. Also be prepared for the questions about what it will really take. Don't sugarcoat the work effort, but make sure it's clear that the benefits outweigh the risks (assuming *you* really feel that is the case).

After all that, be prepared for the "What's next?" question. If they are ready to sign up, then you need to be ready for what has to happen next. Ask them to have conversations with the executives, or find a way to make those conversations possible for you. Ensure that your requests (for the next steps) are tangible—"Could you get me a meeting with the CFO?" or "I need you to help me create a governance council by evangelizing your support of this program."

Finally, the longest path to sponsorship is through the grassroots effort. This entails talking with just about everyone possible about the benefit and value-add of BI to the organization. You may question the value of this type of sponsorship, particularly because of the time investment. I would recommend that if you are able to secure executive or influencer support early on, then move forward. You don't have to wait for grassroots sponsorship to solidify your support before beginning. But the grassroots level of sponsorship provides the BI program with cheerleaders at the level where most employees are. Grassroots support means that the BI program is functioning well enough that anyone in the organization understands the value. Very few things are as powerful as having that kind of support behind an initiative.

These multiple levels of support mean that you are better positioned once the BI program gets underway. Each sponsor type will play a different role for the program, but each role is critical. Once the sponsorship is up and running and the BI program starts its work, it's like a snowball at the top of the hill—it will gain its own momentum.

Why Multiple Levels of Sponsorship Are Recommended

The average chief executive officer keeps his or her job for five to seven years. That means that most of us have experienced a turnover in leadership at our organizations at the highest level. Obviously, when leadership changes, so does the focus on projects, programs, and even the overall vision of the organization. So if you only have one sponsor, what happens if he or she leaves? Significant changes will rock your world if that occurs. The best insurance policy is not to put all of your eggs in one basket. As you are beginning, it is acceptable to have just one sponsor to get your project up and running, but as your program grows and begins to deliver valuable content, it's critical that you expand your sponsorship program.

The value of different levels of sponsorship is simple. The more people in your organization who rely on the content generated by the BI group, the more potential sponsors, supporters, and cheerleaders you have. You'll then be less likely to find yourself without support (or worse, without a budget).

Take advantage of all of the different types of sponsorship. Ensure that you have an influencer on the team, especially because he or she is moving upward and you can probably count on that person once he or she reaches a higher level. Keeping a strong grassroots effort going is vital, too. Perhaps the masses don't have big titles, but they do have the weight of quantity. If enough people support you, and would be vocal about the potential loss of your BI group, the safer you are. This type of diversification for your sponsorship means that you will have time to focus on other things just as important to the BI program.

Losing a Sponsor: The Grieving Process

It happens. Perhaps you were just gaining some traction and all of a sudden the rug is pulled out from under you because your executive sponsor resigns. It's not a good feeling. But before you update your resume, take a few minutes and assess the severity of the situation. First, if the sponsor is still there for a little while (resigning on good terms), set up a short meeting. Ask for help in identifying a successor for sponsorship. Executives don't decide to depart at the drop of a hat, so sponsors have probably been planning what should happen to the BI program postdeparture. If they are conscientious about their responsibilities, they may have already decided on a sponsor replacement, which would be great news for you. If not, it's fair to ask them about a new sponsor and to phrase it so they know you expect them to help find a replacement.

Ideally, your replacement sponsor will wield the same clout and command the same respect in the organization. In addition, recognize that you need to educate the new sponsor much like you educated the original one. Don't assume you can do a "find and replace" on the sponsor name in your documentation and then just move on. Good sponsorship only happens when all your sponsors are well versed in the program.

If the current sponsor doesn't have a succession plan, or left suddenly, then you will have to rely more on your other sponsors to ensure continued support. This is one of the main reasons why you want more than one sponsor. You need that safety net.

Sometimes you can't find a back-up sponsor and you have limited sponsorship from the other areas, so you're in a bit of a pickle. First, don't panic. In the top-10 list of things that kill BI programs, lacking a sponsor for a few weeks does not appear. You have time to reconsider your options, or continue to build up your reputation to help secure a strong sponsor. It's okay to decide to skip a formal "executive sponsor" and continue with the influencer and/or grassroots sponsorship. But ending up with no sponsorship—or very little—spells disaster. Weak grassroots sponsorship won't sustain you if you are being asked tough questions during a budget cycle. That's why an executive sponsor is so critical over the long haul.

Losing a sponsor can be time consuming and distracting. Let me give you a scenario: You identify and finalize your chief medical officer (CMO) as your executive sponsor. He's a bright guy who's been looking at data for more than two decades. He took over the role as CMO about 18 months ago and has since (with a fair amount of frequency) been vocal about his disappointment regarding the lack of data. Your previous sponsor was the chief operations officer, but she left and her replacement wasn't named immediately. She recommended that you approach the CMO. In the beginning it seemed like the perfect partnership, but now all you hear are complaints about the slowness of the process. The CMO is even more vocal about not caring where or how you get the data, "Just get it!" You have attempted to explain to him that "just getting the data" doesn't really work, but his eyes glaze over and he starts scrolling through his email on his BlackBerry. You realize that you have a real problem on your hands. This sponsor is not supportive or helpful, as a matter of fact; in boardroom conversations you have heard that he's planning to "whip the BI group into shape." Now what?

First, you will need to determine what type of understanding the sponsor has of the BI program. Why did he or she agree to sponsor? What was the motivation? For non-BI professionals, you will find two types of people: ones that don't get it, and ones that don't want to get it. The people who don't get it can be taught; the people who don't want to get it can be a real problem. Which one is your executive sponsor? If the sponsor falls into the "don't want to get it" category, you're better off cutting your losses. Start the search for a new executive sponsor and move on. However, if you sense a willingness to learn, then try again and position the conversation in terms the sponsor can understand.

If you are trying to educate the executive sponsors, it's best to start when they have an open mind. If you recall my section about why executives sponsor BI programs, you know you should start going through all of the feedback you have received regarding the value of the BI program. Present that collection of value to the sponsors, touting either the tangible value (such as ROI, discussed in another section), or value in the positive feedback from others. Don't assume that you can just send this information in an email—present it to the executive. You may even want to consider asking someone in the organization who currently endorses the program (such as a manager) to mention his or her support to the sponsor. The crucial thing to remember here is not to write off the executives as impossible just because they don't support you. Perhaps you haven't spent enough time or given them the right reasons to support you. Take the time to do that, and if you've given it the old college try and you still aren't receiving the sponsorship that's imperative for success, move on to someone else.

Keeping Your Sponsor Happy

Happiness for sponsors of a BI program usually hinges on four factors:

1. Kudos received for all of the great things the BI team is doing for the organization
2. High-quality data that supports good decision making for leadership
3. Reasonable expectations
4. Return on investment

The first three are obvious; the last one will take some work. The reason that ROI is an important part of keeping your sponsor happy is that your sponsors, whether they are traditional or influencers, will have to answer some really tough questions about the tangible value BI will bring the organization. If you provide some of this information ahead of time, and as part of the ongoing process for your BI program, your sponsor will thank you. I am going to focus on how to accomplish the last one.

STEP-BY-STEP APPROACH TO CALCULATING ROI Healthcare organizations will likely always be in a position to have to validate their investments, particularly those investments that aren't directly related to clinical care (such as a new MRI machine). Return on investment (ROI) has been elusive for the BI industry. The conundrum is that most companies understand at an intrinsic level that organizing data and providing access to information has value. They have historically supported the exercise based on that intrinsic value. But with the inevitable budget-slashing, BI is on the short list because there has not been an effort to validate the intrinsic value of the data. When there have been efforts to validate it, the difficulty comes in actually getting to a positive ROI. Enterprise BI projects can be expensive. In addition, it is challenging to quantify the value of things like faster reporting and more productive users.

Definition: Return on Investment

In finance, return on investment (ROI) is the ratio of money gained or lost on an investment relative to the amount of money invested. Cost benefit analysis (CBA) is a formal discipline used to help appraise or assess the case for a project or proposal, weighing the total expected costs against the total expected benefits.

So that you'll be prepared for the day when your sponsor asks you to demonstrate the ROI of your BI program, I will:

- Review the ROI analysis for BI.
- Explore tips on finding the hidden value of BI in your organization.
- Explain how to measure the intangible aspects of BI.
- Explain how to position the discussion on value in the context of investment.

Defining variations on the theme of ROI is important. Aspects of the NPV (net present value) and IRR (internal rate of return) can be used in an ROI calculation. In some cases you may be able to replace the cost benefit analysis (CBA) for the ROI, making your work that much easier.

Definition: Net Present Value

Net present value (NPV) is defined as the total present value of a time series of cash flows. It is a standard method for using the time value of money to appraise long-term projects.

Definition: Internal Rate of Return

The internal rate of return (IRR) is a capital budgeting metric used by organizations to decide whether they should make investments. It is an indicator of the efficiency or quality of an investment, as opposed to NPV, which indicates value or magnitude.

If you can't complete your ROI analysis in five steps or fewer, then you should do an ROI analysis on your ROI analysis.

The faster you are able to put a stake in the ground regarding the quantifiable value of your program, the faster you can get to proving it, which is the most valuable aspect of the analysis.

Step 1: Define the Business Goals of the Project

Simply stated, a goal is any request by the business that can be supported by an enterprise data warehouse through a BI layer. Although this is a broad definition, a true enterprise BI program should be delivering business value to all aspects of the organization. State the goal in terms of success, such as "Provide the appeals department a personalized portal with predefined reports." This shouldn't be difficult to find, although you may find it difficult to quantify. If you review the case study of Blue Cross Blue Shield of Kansas City and their best practices award, the way they found a 332 percent return was by measuring the business use of the BI program.

Step 2: Measure the Goals

When defining the goals, strive to make them measurable. To continue with our prestated goal of "Provide the appeals department a personalized portal with predefined reports," the measurement aspect of that goal is the availability of the portal, the active use of the portal and the number of times the predefined reports have been run. These are success criteria because they make employees of the appeals department more productive. Generally avoid statements like "Improve customer satisfaction," and use a better goal such as "Improve customer satisfaction by 1 percent each quarter, for a cumulative change of 4 percent for the year." This way, as each quarter passes you can measure your progress and avoid any unhappy surprises at the end of the year. This also allows you to make a mid-year course correction

ROI = (NPV of Savings/Initial Investment + Maintenance Cost) * 100

FIGURE 4.3 ROI Calculation

(if things aren't going as planned) by either restating the goal or revising the survey that measures the satisfaction.

Step 3: Determine the Investment

The second major part of the ROI calculation are the investments. These can be significant depending on whether you have to buy software and hardware. Each organization has guidelines for what you can capitalize or amortize. Because the cost can be significant, it is recommended to amortize the investment over the first two or three years of the program.

Step 4: Calculate the ROI

Once you have all the data, calculating the ROI percentage is easy. Simply apply the data to the calculation (see Figure 4.3).

Step 5: Program Evaluation

Set up a plan to consistently measure and validate the ROI analysis. Critically important in determining the long-term value of the program is periodically reviewing your ROI analysis and seeking to improve it through better goal definition, improved metrics, and so on. Your organization's vision and mission are not stagnant and your ROI analysis shouldn't be either.

THE INTANGIBLES: MEASURING THE VALUE OF SOFT RETURN ON INVESTMENT Often referred to as the soft aspect of an ROI analysis, the intangibles will likely determine the difference between positive and negative ROI for your program. The trick here is to make the immeasurable measurable. Every intangible metric has some aspect that is quantifiable. You may have to break it down into a smaller piece of consumable data, but somewhere the intangible has a metric that can be measured.

We all understand the potential value in goals like faster reporting, better management information, better decision making, more productive users, improved patient satisfaction, faster decisions, opportunity cost, efficiency gains, and better risk profiling for disease management, but the challenge has always been to measure them well enough so that your executives do not question your methodology or analysis. In a recent conversation with a CFO about an ROI analysis, he questioned my methodology regarding a calculation I made attributing a percentage of sales to the BI program. The calculation made my ROI positive; without it, it was negative for more than a three-year period. Even though I had discounted the value of the intangible metric (we only allocated 2 percent of a sale) and had validated the assumption with the VP of sales, backed by our "Lost Sales Surveys," it was still removed from the calculation. It's important to not only quantify what you can but have a strong business case and reasoning behind including it in the calculation. Even then, you may not like the outcome.

Some goals are easier to measure than others (see Table 4.1). For example, measuring your customers' satisfaction and how it changes over time is reasonably straightforward. Usually this is done through a survey. The potential impact a BI program has on customer satisfaction has to be agreed on at the time the survey is created to ensure the most appropriate questions are asked.

Other things, like better decision making, are much more amorphous concepts. "Good decisions usually have systematically assembled data and analysis behind them" (Davenport, 2007). It's still difficult to measure the cost of a bad decision, or compare it to the value of a good decision. Only with proper use of your organization's BI are you able to quantify the value an informed decision delivers. For example, if you enter a new

TABLE 4.1 Goals and Measurement

Type of Goal	How to Measure It
Patient Satisfaction	Add questions to existing survey asking about satisfaction associated with information available electronically.
Faster Reporting	Revenue cycle management would be impacted, because the faster finance can get the information, the faster they can submit accounts receivable.
Improved Risk Profiling for Disease Management	Quantify the improved ability to identify risk-based profiles by the improvement in care delivery. This will be a long-term measurement.
Staff Efficiency Gains	Using data to determine staff efficiencies can be measured through both improved care to patients (measured through patient satisfaction) and reduced staffing costs.

market, you are able to analyze the metrics associated with that action in order to make a more informed decision as well as measure the result of that decision—that is, the increased revenue and market penetration. With that said, it is still best practice to discount the impact of the intangibles between 10 and 40 percent. This risk adjustment provides the opportunity to include these important factors in your analysis without putting your investment at risk (Pisello, 2009).

Opportunity Cost

Opportunity cost is *the* most underconsidered aspect of ROI for BI programs and, arguably, the most noteworthy benefit of BI. In certain industries access to data or the ability to provide access to data is a major competitive differentiator. An "intelligent enterprise"—one that uses BI to advance its business—is better able to predict how future economic and market changes

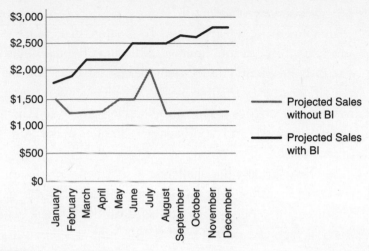

FIGURE 4.4 Opportunity Cost

will affect its business. Such an organization is able to adapt to the new changes in order to gain (Bogza, 2008). Your health-care organization's ability to manage a BI program could mean the difference between losing groups and gaining them—a very quantifiable metric! Figure 4.4 demonstrates the difference, as explained in terms of "sales" but could easily be attributed to gaining groups or, as in the potential world of health information exchanges, patients, and members.

The easiest part of an ROI analysis is the tangible measurements, usually the mean cost elements such as the cost of hardware, software, and full-time equivalents (FTEs). You may be able to find a couple of tangible benefits for your ROI calculation, such as the reduced cost of software (if you switch pricing models or just software itself). Reduced FTE is a benefit to your bottom line. If you can't (or are not willing) to reduce FTE, you may also see a benefit in reducing the pedestrian tasks of preparing data so those same FTEs will have time to complete value add analytics.

To take full advantage of an ROI analysis, first define your business goals, making sure to consider the entire enterprise your program serves. Once your business goals are stated, you must plan to measure against them. To do this, make sure you take into account both the tangible and intangible elements of the goal. For the intangible elements, consider breaking them into smaller, more measureable metrics. Finally, actively manage the analysis and metrics and run the analysis twice a year. As your business grows and your metrics change, make sure to adjust accordingly.

These steps simplify the challenge associated with completing an ROI analysis for a healthcare BI program, but the days of getting your BI program funded based on the intrinsic value of managing data are gone. As a BI practitioner it is your responsibility to complete a comprehensive ROI analysis. Your sponsors will expect it and your leadership will prize an ROI analysis done well.

Each tenet of healthcare BI plays a significant role in your program's success. With the other tenets, though, there are checklists and standard methods that can help you improve data quality or bring your technology up-to-date. But leadership of a BI program is different—it involves a considerable amount of art (along with the practical rigors). Without good leadership, your sponsorship of the program won't grow. Without good leadership, the organization may not see the value as quickly or easily. Without good leadership, it will be more difficult to build the BI team. It's true that BI leadership isn't the be-all and end-all; you can't just have a great leader and nothing else. But, when there is nothing else, having a great leader means that you can create something great.

Notes

1105 Media. (2010, August 15). *TDWI*. Retrieved December 2, 2011, from The Data Warehousing Institute, A Division of 1105 Media: http://tdwi .org/pages/best-practices-awards/tdwi-best-practice-awards-2010-winners .aspx.

Bogza, R. Z. (2008). Automation, Quality and Testing. *Robotics*, Volume 1, Issue 22-25, Pages 146–151.

Tuckman, B. (1965). "Developmental Sequence in Small Groups," *Psychological Bulletin*, Vol. 63, No. 6, Pages 384–399.

Glen, P., and D. H. Maister (2002). *Leading Geeks: How to Manage and Lead the People Who Deliver Technology*. Jossey-Bass.

Pisello, T. (2009, March). *Tom Pisello: ROI Guy*. Retrieved March 2010, from Alinean: www.tompiselloroiguy.blogspot.com.

Davenport, T. H., and J. G. Harris (2007). *Competing on Analytics: The New Science of Winning*. Boston: Harvard Business School Press.

CHAPTER 5

Technology and Architecture

If, by some chance, you are an IT person (say a database administrator) I'm afraid this chapter is not meant for you. I am not about to address the technical pros and cons of columnar databases or the importance of the cloud. This chapter is about enabling the team to build the right technology and architecture to support the business needs of the BI program. For those of you that aren't technical, this chapter covers the basics of what you need to understand to support these efforts. So, the question may be: "What is important to understand?" As a business leader you will likely never become an expert at any of these concepts, nor should you. The most important thing that you can do is hire good people you trust and stay well-informed about the impact of your decisions on the long-term success of the program. For IT professionals, it's our duty to ensure that we explain concepts in terms that business leaders can understand. The goal is to ensure that they understand the impact of any decision they make, in their terms. Part of that effort has to be educational, but the other part of it has to be focused on the predetermined goals of the program. In other words, if we are asking our executives to support a decision we need to make in platform architecture, we have to, first, make sure that the business leader knows what platform architecture is and, second, that they understand the impact to things end-users care about such as performance, availability, security, and accuracy.

Technology and Architecture:
A Business Definition

Technology could cover anything from the iPhone that you have in your pocket (or the Kindle that you are reading this on), to a server in your building. For the purposes of this section, technology refers to the hardware and software associated with business intelligence (BI).

Similarly, architecture may be a new term for you in the context of IT. When you think about how most people understand architecture—blueprints for houses and remodels—that applies to our uses as well. Simply, architecture for BI is planning out the use, allocation, and investment in technology (software and hardware) for application in a BI program.

In the opening pages of this book I related a story about a less-than-optimized data model that led to many hours with lawyers. Ever since that situation I have evangelized the importance of a data model. I think that perhaps more than any other industry, healthcare must focus its time and effort on ensuring that the data model is structured appropriately. About a year ago I had a conversation with a well-known data modeler. I was requesting his assistance with a client of mine. He said to me in no uncertain terms that he prefers not to work with healthcare data because it's so "messy" and "convoluted." I was surprised by his response, not just because he was so well-known but because he readily admitted that he would avoid it at all costs. I thought to myself, if he's avoiding it where does that leave the rest of us? Thankfully, I have since found an equally knowledgeable data modeler who doesn't shy away from the challenge. What I have learned from him is simple: The relationships in the data are essential; get those right and most other things fall into place. The other helpful thing I learned is that you don't have to do absolutely everything right away. Avoid the "big bang" approach to data warehousing, where you attempt to model every possible data point into an enterprise data model in one big project. This approach is fraught with risk. The best approach is to identify the relationships, pick a report or dashboard that will bring the organization value, and build from there. If you focus on value and the relationships in the data, you won't miss anything. Don't attempt to design and build everything all at once; the pressure associated with the short time frame means you will most likely miss something important. Take the time to ensure that you understand the business needs and what drives them. You also have to make sure that you are prepared to adapt when the business changes, because changes happen all the time.

What does that really mean if you are a business leader? You certainly aren't about to sit down and start modeling the data yourself (although I have seen this). I have many conversations with frustrated business leaders about IT. What I hear most frequently is that business leaders fear what they don't understand. Business leaders are concerned that IT is "pulling the wool over our eyes" when it comes to the work it actually takes or the complexity of the work. Architecture is sometimes used as the scapegoat for this, because BI programs require many layers of architecture. The word *architecture* can be overused, leading to confusion and, in many cases, distrust. As we reviewed in the business definition of architecture, we use this term to cover the planning, allocation, and investment of the technology associated with BI. Because there can be a significant investment, and the technology is the method by which the information is delivered to the business user, it's crucial to ensure that your technology is architected to support the BI program.

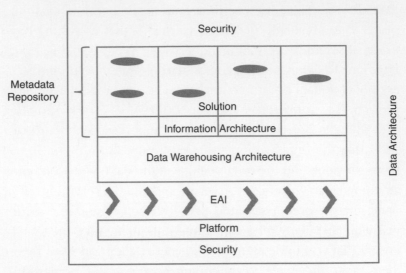

FIGURE 5.1 Architecture for BI Programs

As you can see from Figure 5.1, there are many factors and interplay associated with building a strong BI program. If someone says "architecture" to you, they are probably referring to one of these. As a business leader, if an IT person refers to an architectural decision or consequences, you can ask them what type of architecture they are referring to. Okay, so business folks are from Mars and IT folks are from Venus. Let's move on.

The "Abilities": Scalability, Usability, Repeatability, Flexibility

Nearly 10 years ago I was sitting in an office with a co-worker trying to find the words to describe the work effort we had going on. The team, his team, had built a BI suite of tools and I was the product manager. We wanted to do the next round of planning for the product to evolve it from what it was to a bigger, better version. We realized that what we needed to build

TABLE 5.1 The "Abilities"

Scalability	Usability	Repeatability	Flexibility
Data Architecture	EAI	SDLC for BI	Platform Architecture
Platform Architecture	Security Architecture	RFP Process	Data Architecture
EAI	Information Architecture	Information Architecture	Solution Architecture

was a product that was able to scale to the data we planned on using (we weren't even talking about terabytes yet). We needed it to be user-friendly; many of our end-users were not that computer savvy. We realized that we needed to articulate a method that allowed us to build and modify the product in a repeatable, consistent way. But most important to us, the product had to be flexible. We knew that based on the market our ability to evolve this product continuously over time was going to be central to our success. So, we came up with the "abilities," the descriptors of what we needed the product to represent (see Table 5.1).

Today, these abilities are the same things we need to think about as we are building the technology and architecture for our BI program. Each of these descriptors represents a key part of the technical structure that helps a BI program succeed. If you aren't able to scale, your performance will suffer and so will user adoption. If you aren't able to make the front end user-friendly, it will impact your user base; if you can't make it flexible to allow for improvements over time, you won't be able to support the dynamic business of healthcare; and if you don't articulate a repeatable process for improvements, executive support for your budget will wane. Each of the abilities has different aspects that can impact multiple levels of the architecture. As you go through these sections you will notice that they repeat, but the function to address them is quite different. Really, these abilities represent the same thing today as they did 10 years ago. They represent a platform for success.

Scalability

Definition

Scalabilty is the ability of an application or product (hardware or software) to continue to function well when it is changed in size or volume in order to meet a user need (TechTarget, 2000).

Preparing for Growth

Architecturally, there are three major areas where we can and should consider scalability. The first is platform architecture. That is the hardware and software that we purchase to support our programs. The second is enterprise application integration (EAI), which is the architecture that moves the data between the transactional systems and the data warehouse. This is where we can manage the reusability of the data through metadata, which will allow us improved ability to scale. Finally, there is data architecture, the structure and relationships of the data created to support usage. In all three of these instances there are things we can do to ensure that we have the scalability to grow the BI environment for increasing usage.

Let's address the platform architecture first. Scalability allows us to maintain a consistent level of performance regardless of changes and growth. When first getting started with platform architecture it is crucial for us to "get it right the first time." From a platform perspective the best way to do that is to consider how much activity the system will experience. We call this usage concurrency; in other words, how many people will be on the system at the same time doing similar activities. You will need to purchase hardware to scale to this amount. As you consider how much you want to scale to, keep in mind that you should have a little "fudge factor" in there. You don't want to scale to what your usage is now if you're planning a 10 percent increase next year. Planning ahead is an insurance policy that you can easily obtain. This isn't the time to skimp either—buy the servers you need to ensure that performance you want. It's a bit like buying the right insurance policy. You may never need it, but when you do, you sure are glad it's there.

Relationships Change

Scaling in the context of data architecture is a bit more complex. There is a balance there of the functional things you can do with the data model so it performs and the limitations of how you want to use the data. We have talked a lot about relationships in the context of healthcare data. What I mean by this is how the data relates to one another. For example, the relationship between a patient and his or her primary care physician is a many-to-one relationship; that is, the physician has many patients but the patient has only one primary care physician (PCP). Then you consider specialties. The patient may see many specialists and the specialists see many patients; that, is a many-to-many relationship (see Figure 5.2). It has no bearing on the PCP relationship but there are times when you need to understand who the patient is seeing (i.e., when did they see their PCP and what specialists did they see last). A patient is a member of a health plan, but a member isn't always a patient. These are the types of things that data modelers are interested in. How these relationships are structured architecturally can impact performance, because generally speaking the

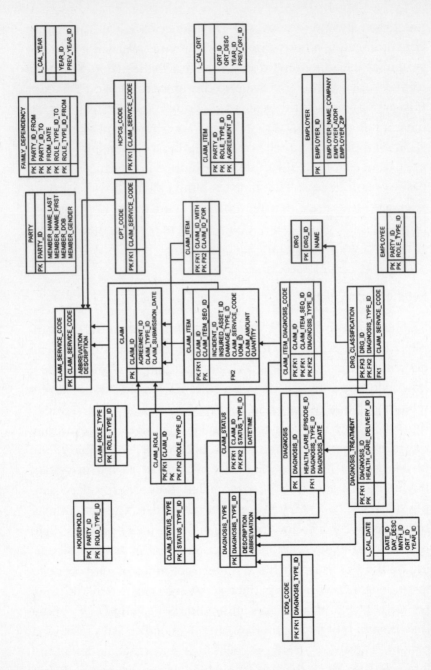

FIGURE 5.2 Data Relationships

108

more "relationships"—or in query-speak "joins"—the longer the report will take to return once you hit "run." But even that's not black and white because many things can be done to ensure that a query with many joins returns in short order.

Regardless of the complexity associated with data modeling, one thing is certain, you as a business leader need to stay engaged enough to ensure that the business needs are being met. You may delegate this to someone closer to the data, such as an analyst, but make sure that the data modeler is presenting the data model in a conceptual model. A data modeler told me once that if a businessperson can't look at the conceptual model and easily determine what business they are in, then something is wrong. Conceptual models are drawings of how your data relates to one another and they should absolutely reflect the organizational needs of the data.

Change Happens

Finally, for scalability we discuss EAI. We discuss EAI in the context of usability as well, but for scalability we are most interested in the part of EAI that makes the data warehouse "source system agnostic." What this means in business terms is that we can add or change any of our transactional systems (i.e., our electronic health record [EHR] or financial systems) and not impact our data warehouse. This is a big benefit for most data warehouse projects because in the lifetime of the data warehouse, a source system is likely to be changed. If you tie yourself too tightly to that source system, rather than putting a layer in place like EAI to buffer your data warehouse, any change, even small changes, can mean a significant down time, or worse, changes in the data itself. EAI creates a process and a platform for which you base all of the data movement into your data warehouse. That layer of architecture protects the output of data, so you can change your input while maintaining your output. The best analogy for this is car parts. No matter how many times you change your battery, put on high-performance tires, or soup up the engine, you will always have a Chevy Impala. The same applies here; you can go from Great Plains to Lawson, from McKesson to Allscripts, and we will always have the same data warehouse for users to access.

Usability

> ### Definition
>
> Usability is the ease of use and learnability of a human-made object. The object of use can be a software application, website, book, tool, machine, process, or anything a human interacts with (Wikipedia, 2010).

In Chapter 6 we discuss the general user interface (GUI) at some length. Usability from an architecture perspective is quite different though. It may be the best-kept secret in BI that much of the BI program's usability, specifically the data, comes from "behind the scenes." Our ability to prepare the data for consumption has a lot to do with data governance, but the architectural concepts that support data governance such as EAI, information architecture and security architecture play a key role as well.

Knowledge Is Power: Support Metadata

Starting with EAI, again we learn that the process and platform provided by EAI allows us to improve user adoption by creating the baseline for metadata management. We discuss metadata in Chapter 6, but for our purposes in this section we need to understand how metadata creates the framework that not only allows us the scalability and source system agnostic benefits but also the ability to improve user adoption.

Metadata improves user adoption by ensuring that all your end-users know exactly what data they are using, how it's calculated, and where it comes from. The importance of this is obvious when you first go live with a new system, particularly if users are more used to having to access data in a much more "hands-on" way; in other words, they are used to writing queries and pulling data from tables with the associated joins themselves. Metadata provides users context for the data, usually in a hover box (referred to as a *tool tip*). The system will now provide that buffer for them, but most end-users are uncomfortable with that in the beginning. The metadata management layer as supported by EAI helps by giving users the transparency they need, such as where the data is coming from and how it's calculated. The long-term benefits from that metadata management layer are the scalability and source system agnosticism discussed in the section under scalability.

Security makes systems more usable. It provides us with the assurances we need to use the system but not abuse the system. As noted in Figure 5.3, security is a frame that wraps around all aspects of the architecture.

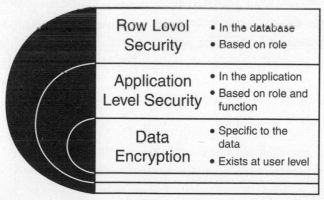

FIGURE 5.3 Many Layers of Security

How to Avoid Lawyers: Secure Your Data

Security should never be in just one spot. The more redundancy you have, the less likely you are to have an issue. Here's another story that involves lawyers (you may think I don't like them but it's not true, they have saved my bacon more than I like to admit). This time it involves inadvertent PHI (personal health information) disclosures; those pesky little situations that lead to hours and hours of analyzing data to determine who had access to what. Luckily for me, at the time we didn't have exposure to patients, but other businesses inadvertently received access to data that wasn't theirs. The main reason was that our security only existed at the application level. We had a good BI application but our security protocol never extended to the data warehouse itself, or within the solution architecture. In all reality, organizations should have security at the application, which resides within the solution architecture and there should always (*always*!) be security at the database level. Then if there is a failure at the application level (in our case, it was when we migrated from test to production environments), at a minimum the database security prevents end-users from accessing data they shouldn't see. There are other helpful safeguards that organizations can implement, such as encryption. However you proceed, you must know that security has to exist in many different places within your architecture to make your system truly secure. Security improves usability, not the other way around, because when people feel secure about the data they are more inclined to use it.

From Data to Decisions

Finally, for usability we discuss information architecture. Information architecture is much like it sounds; it is how we get from just data to information that improves business decisions. The way we do that in a BI system is to apply business rules.

Business rules are the things that we know and understand about the data that makes the data more informative to our decision making. For example, when you want to create a value of all patients with Diabetes Type II, you have to include the diagnostic codes that equal that diagnosis. That's a business rule. There is no single way to determine a diagnosis of Diabetes Type II in the data, but when you apply the business rule of ICD-9 codes to the data, there is. Many other examples of business rules exist for healthcare. As a matter of fact, healthcare is one of those industries that requires lots of business rules to ensure the usefulness of the information and that's how information architecture can help. In many cases, information architecture, or the method in which you apply these business rules is called *extract, transform, and load* (ETL). In the opening pages of the book I revealed how important I think ETL is to the value of healthcare data. ETL is like the special sauce that makes regular data into useful data. Like the McDonald's version, we need to know exactly what is in that special sauce. ETL applies the business rules and supports much of our data quality efforts. Good ETL supports your program goals.

Like most things, there is a good way and a bad way to do ETL. Because of the complexities associated with the business rules for healthcare and the application of data quality standards it is a very good idea to make sure that you think about it in terms of architecture.

Ten Best Practices for Healthcare ETL

1. Apply a repeatable process

    Just like any other best practices, we need to follow software development life-cycle best practices for ETL as well as for code reusability, robustness, flexibility, and manageability. A Software Development

Lifecycle (SDLC) will provide a repeatable method in which to apply business rules and data quality standards as well as address issues for error handling. Standards that should be created and followed for any successful ETL project include: naming conventions, error handling and notification, reusability, metadata management, and failure and recovery processes. There will be more information about how to use an SDLC for BI in the next section on repeatability.

2. Provide a strategic view

The ETL project team should have exposure to the strategic information goals of the organization data and integration initiatives so that they can design conforming dimensions and conforming facts to ensure that the growth of the project aligns with the strategic plans of the organization. Without this enterprise-wide view, your ETL plans may miss an integral piece of the puzzle for future development and therefore require rework. To ensure that this doesn't happen, identify a resource on the ETL team who can interact with the project team to ensure that all design requirements are heard firsthand (a good practice from Agile methods).

3. Data profiling and data quality

A clean data source will require minimal transformations, while a "noisy" data source will require extensive data transformations. "Noisy" data is data that doesn't abide by the data quality standards set by the organization. For example, in a field that has the standard of four-character numeric value with a decimal point in the third place, you find a value of 9.999999999. When this occurs often, it is considered "noisy" data.

It is important to determine what level of data quality is expected from the source system. By applying data profiling, the ETL team may reveal noisy data sources that cannot be supported by an ETL process and need some additional ETL processes to handle the requirements. By performing data profiling, the ETL team may determine some additional data quality ETL processes to overcome the noisy data sources to fulfill customers' requirements.

4. Utilize a data staging area

You should store data temporarily in a staging area so that it mimics the sources system for data controls, quick/frequent look-ups, and insulates the data warehouse repository from source system changes. This staging area also helps with audit controls and recovery times if there is a job failure.

5. Encourage reusable transformations

A transformation is a key building block of an ETL process, so defining adequate standards and encouraging the ETL developers to design reusable transformations will save time, money, and avoid errors.

6. Keep it timely

Here, data timeliness, also referred to as data latency, denotes to how quickly the source data must be delivered for end-user consumption. Consequently, it is a good idea to determine this well in advance to avoid latency issues that ultimately may lead to poor end-user adoption of the data warehouse.

There has long been debate among BI practitioners in healthcare about data latency. Many question the value of real-time data in healthcare because so much data transformation has to take place for the data to be useful to the average person. "Zero latency" is a popular concept. It allows data to be appropriately transformed but gets it to the data warehouse in an expeditious manner, rather than waiting for the next day or week to receive data.

7. Handling ETL errors gracefully

Errors will happen. When they do, it is critical for the ETL architects to have created a design that handles ETL errors on initiation of an ETL job and allows for a restart automatically when errors occur. A process for addressing these errors is necessary because errors can impact deadlines, require expensive rework cycles, or produce inaccurate data into the data warehouse. Records that fail the business rules should be written to a file for the business owners or data stewards to investigate. This should prompt a change of business rules to account for the new information and for future reprocessing.

8. ETL testing

The accuracy of the data in the data warehouse is imperative. When data is integrated from different sources there is a chance of error. Thus, it is important to involve the testing team along with the development team as early as during the requirements-gathering stage so that they can define the high-level test approach, test estimation, test plan creation, test case creation, and test case execution.

9. Knowledge of ETL tools

Using an ETL tool without understanding its capabilities and ETL processes is a major issue we have seen in many data warehousing and business intelligence projects. To be successful, it is important to have experienced and knowledgeable ETL architects, designers, and developers on the team. Constantly review the ETL team's training needs and provide the ETL tool knowledge appropriately.

10. Compliance requirements

Healthcare has some of the most stringent regulations of any industry. The proposed ETL solution must plan for the compliance requirements placed on it by state and federal regulations, industry best practices, standards, and guidelines. Ensure that you have a method for audit controls, which require the ability to track the data to the original source and the original state of the data (Rao Nemani, 2011).

Repeatability

Definition

The definition for repeatability for our purposes is specific to process repeatability. It is the things that we do to ensure that we can repeat a process again with consistency and high-quality deliverables.

Process for Success

Much of what we do in BI is repeated. For the first year of a BI project everything will be new, but after that everything old is new again. Therefore, the smart move is to create and document the repeatable processes that get you through your first year to help you excel in the years beyond. That repeatable process is

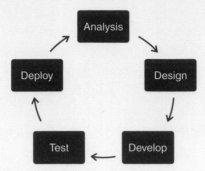

FIGURE 5.4 Software Development Lifecycle

often referred to as an *SDLC* or *Software Development Lifecycle*. We are going to rebrand this to *BIDLC* or *BI Development Lifecycle*, but the steps are the same and you only need one (SDLC or BIDLC). See Figure 5.4.

For each of these steps, the activities must be done to pass through to the next stage; these are often referred to as *stage-gates*. The BIDLC implies a strong connection to waterfall development. The waterfall methodology means that at the end of each stage there is a hand-off, often through documentation, to the next team. Between analysis and design, you hand your business requirements to designers and walk away. As a business analyst you are done with your job. You will certainly be available for questions but you are no longer on the hook for the result of the design that is the designer's job. This continues through the life cycle from analysts to designer to developer to tester. What you end up getting is a bad case of can-and-string telephone (see Figure 5.5).

You may notice that nowhere in this process do we discuss the people who are actually requesting the report or dashboard, the end-users. Not until they are at the end of the can, getting a different message than what they sent. The only value that a BIDLC provides is the structure to repeat a process that is useful to the end-result.

FIGURE 5.5 Can-and-String Lifecycle

One of the challenges with delivering content for BI is that many users aren't able to articulate their information needs until you are through the development life cycle, when it's too late. When you ask early on in the SDLC method, users will just simply say "give me the data," which isn't what they mean, but they aren't sure how to express their needs until they have something tangible to respond to. In a standard SDLC/waterfall development methodology, you get "done" creating what you thought they asked for, and when they get it they ask for something else or something more. For example, you give them a report on average bed days and they look at that (for a minute or a day) and return it to you asking if it's possible to break it down by unit and provider. You are at the end of the development cycle, so that means that you have to do the project all over again. If you had gained this information earlier it would have had less of an impact (see Figure 5.6).

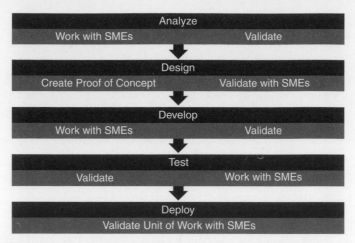

FIGURE 5.6 Business Intelligence Development Lifecycle

This is why agile methodologies for business intelligence work so well. The seminal book on this topic is *Agile Data Warehousing* (Hughes, 2008), and it redefines how to deliver value in the context of business intelligence and data warehousing.

When Good Processes Go Bad

Sometimes when you are working on a project, particularly a large project, certain people go a little crazy trying to document the repeatable processes such as code reviews, report development methods, and so on via an SDLC. A few years ago as I was working on a BI deployment, the project manager and business analyst got together and decided that they would build out a thorough step-wise approach to the SDLC we were using. Complete with swim-lanes and "actors," the two created a 42-page (no exaggeration) process that we were all supposed to follow. Needless to say, most of us spent our time trying to print out and tape the visual together rather than actually doing the work. The massive structure was soon streamlined to the key activities that had to happen at each of the stages for all major participants. It's a good warning though: documentation for documentation's sake doesn't improve the repeatability of an activity.

RFP PROCESSES TO PROCURE THE RIGHT TECHNOLOGY   At some point in your BI evolution you will have to buy a product. In this case, it's software. There are many best practices written for how to purchase software. There are also a number of holdovers from days when BI software packages varied significantly. Allow me to shatter one of the myths that most people hold dear: Most BI products can do the job. It's true, regardless of your allegiance or preferences, most BI products have comparable functions that get the job done. What come next are the subtleties, and some of those subtleties can make or break your project.

So, when you use the old holdover method of purchasing software because that's the way you've always done it, you are likely wasting a great deal of time and money. The focus for the request for proposal/request for information (RFP/RFI) approach was always to ferret out the details that aren't obvious in the marketing brochures that companies revere. But if most of the products can do what you need them to do, then you need to focus on what you need to do, preferences of IT staff (or more importantly, capabilities of IT staff), and your long-term vision for the program.

I am not saying that you have to throw away your entire methodology and start over. There are generally good parts of an RFP/RFI method. But I do recommend that you turn the process on its ear a bit. For example, many RFPs focus on the basic capabilities of the products: the "Can you do this" type of question. The answers to those are easily found on the product's website or by talking to other customers. You don't need to spend countless hours and pages and pages of questions on the basics. You simply make sure that any vendor you invite meets those baseline criteria. In other words, do your homework first. Sometimes it is easier to ask those questions in RFPs because you are busy, but if you spend time doing the homework first, you are not only better prepared to evaluate products for the next phase, you also put the emphasis on the most important part of the process, which is evaluating similar products for their ability to address your future-focused needs.

Think about it like buying a car. With all of the information available online today, you would never walk blindly into a car dealership and point to a pretty red car and say, "How much for that one?" Many times, with RFPs that's exactly what you are doing. You end up focusing on the things that the vendors want you to focus on. I have seen some great RFPs that are good at getting to the core of the organization's needs, but I have responded to many more that ask if we can email reports. Does a car have wheels? When buying a car you will first decide some basic criteria: size, safety, performance, gas mileage, and budget. Then you select the wants: sunroof, sound-system, leather seats, heated seats, and so on. As you begin your research online you only look at the cars that offer the basic criteria and bypass the rest. Then you have the opportunity to concisely evaluate the cars that have your "wants" and potentially more, depending on your budget.

If you bought a car using the traditional RFP approach you may well end up comparing a truck, SUV, and a sedan because you asked if they all had wheels (i.e., can it email reports?). This can be a challenge for many organizations getting started with BI because you don't know what you don't know. Bringing in a vendor you trust to help you through the process is an excellent way to fill that gap. Rely on the vendor's expertise in the area and use it to help narrow down the number of organizations to which you send your RFP. Then, when you send out an RFP, you are prepared to evaluate based on the long-term needs of your organization. You may be asking: What does long term or future-focused mean? Continuing our analogy, if you're planning a family, you probably aren't looking at two-seater cars. If you are planning to move north, you probably aren't looking at convertibles. For BI software, you ask the vendors about emailing reports because that's how you do it today. They all say "Yes, I can!" But what if your executives recently decided in a strategic planning session that they wanted to enable mobile access to information so that the geographically diverse workforce would be less tied to their inbox? You asked a question about today, when what you really need to know about is tomorrow. This can be a costly mistake.

It's a best practice for RFPs that you reach out to the broader organization to ensure that you understand what they need in order to fully adopt the BI product. Don't assume you know just because you have worked there for years. You don't want to be surprised after an expensive purchase and implementation only to learn that your assumptions weren't accurate.

In the appendix is an RFI/RFP template that you can use for these purposes. Some sections are completed to guide you, but you should change the criteria section to meet the needs of your organization. The 10-step process for product acquisition is:

1. Confirm the need for product and set budget.
2. Create the cross-functional steering committee, or adapt the governance committee for the purpose.
3. Interview and secure help from a BI consulting firm (optional).
4. Interview stakeholders for criteria.
5. Complete independent research of BI products.

6. Create RFP.
7. Send RFP.
8. Assess responses from RFP.
9. Invite two to three vendors to demonstrate capabilities.
10. Make final decision.

Interviewing stakeholders to determine their criteria can be really challenging. It's natural to focus on what is done today, rather than what you would like in the coming years. And if you are new to this, it's really hard to understand what is possible. I recommend to organizations that they consider doing a discovery session with a comparable organization that is further along the BI maturity scale to understand what's possible. You would most likely have to rely on a consulting firm to help you with this effort, but there are other ways, including researching how other companies are doing it or asking vendors to help, which can be a slippery slope. Just remember that they are there to sell you their software. They aren't bad people but their incentives aren't aligned to help you better understand the BI industry or what's possible; they are motivated to sell their software.

Once you have a good understanding of what is possible, then you need to decide how to define what your organization wants or needs from a BI product. Make sure to ask the questions that dive into your organizations needs and wants. For example, if you are looking at a mobile deployment, it's important to understand security, application, and hardware implications. If you want to deploy only on the BlackBerry platform then be sure to ask specifically about the vendor's ability to support that platform. Most mobile mechanisms also deploy via the web, so it's important to understand the differences between the two platforms.

You can create a scale of importance or assign weight to certain capabilities over others. For example, if you are particularly interested in high-level data visualizations and enterprise deployment but care less about "ad-hoc" reports, you could weight the visualizations and deployment as having more importance over ad hoc capabilities (something you need but doesn't have to be sophisticated).

Don't Do It This Way

I was working with an organization that had purchased a BI product three years prior. They had followed all of the best practices associated with buying any IT software by creating a steering committee of both IT and business and an RFP of the primary features. The RFP went out to a whole bunch of vendors and the steering committee recommended a purchase. However, the CIO decided to go another way and purchased a product that she was familiar with but had scored rather low on the assessment. The results were catastrophic. Most of her organization felt ignored and angry. They eventually left, and the product was never adopted by the organization as a whole. It was a costly mistake, one that in the end cost her her job.

The importance of the process of an RFP is to make sure that everyone is brought into the process and the method of purchasing the product. This is certainly important for a capital investment but also particularly important to user adoption.

Proof of Concept Best Practices

I'm going to let you in on a secret. Vendors hate RFPs and proof of concepts (POC). It's not because they don't think they can meet the requirements but because they are expensive. When I was a director of BI and doing an RFP, I got upset at the vendor organizations that were giving me a hard time about responding to the RFP and then being invited to do the POC. I thought they would be thrilled, but they were not. A couple of the organizations even declined to participate! The nerve.

What you should know is that some vendors and consulting firms will not, under most circumstances, respond to a cold RFP. Here's why: The return on investment for cold RFPs (*cold* being defined as having no previous knowledge or relationship with the requesting organization) are almost always an exercise in futility. The win rate is less than 10 percent. That means that 90 percent of the time the effort to respond to the RFP is wasted. The ROI improves slightly for a POC, but not drastically so.

The best method for ensuring good participation, so that you as an organization can do a fair job assessing products, is to spend the time with the vendors of interest and help them to understand what you are trying to achieve. That information should be consistent across all the vendors, in other words don't tell one vendor one thing and a different vendor another. Be forthright, honest, and transparent with your process and most vendors will do what they can to win your business. The further you hold them at a distance, the less likely you are to get a good degree of participation. I don't advocate for giving them the world, just what's salient to the process. For example, never let the "winner" know that they are the winner, even if you really aren't considering anyone else. You want them on their toes for negotiation. You need to get the price that will make you feel confident that you made the right choice, but don't beat them up too badly. They want your business, but if they feel like they were taken advantage of it will start your relationship off on a tenuous note.

Believe it or not, the majority of the work for a proof of concept falls on your lap. If you really want to be able to compare apples to apples then you have to spend the time deciding what you want the vendors to do, and then you have to prepare for them to do it. This requires a lot of documentation, data relationships, data definitions, presentation preferences, and so on. If you don't have the appetite for doing the documentation you can't ask vendors to do a POC. They will have a hard time being successful and you will have a hard time comparing apples to apples. The best way to know what vendors will need to do the POC is to take a step back and think about what you want to see the product do. Assume that they have no knowledge of healthcare, and they certainly have no knowledge of your data or data structures. Therefore you have to document everything. The other alternative is to send them a small amount of data for them to use for a POC. Often that isn't an option as organizations want to assess how much effort it is to connect the product to their data, but it is an easier way to determine how the product works.

What Works?

If you are looking to do your due diligence for purchasing a BI tool but don't really have time to do an elaborate request for proposal and proof of concept, here's a good method of doing the work.

- **Do your homework.** Research the available products and their pros and cons. Use analyst reports like Gartner and Forrester.
- **Decide on the top three.** Invite the vendors in for a discussion individually. Ask them to prepare for an exploratory conversation with you. The agenda should include about an hour for your organization and an hour for the vendor organization. In the hour for your organization explain what you do, how you do it, the drivers that brought you to BI, and discuss timelines and budget constraints (whether that be a timing issue or a dollar issue).

- **Ask for industry knowledge.** Ensure that the vendors are prepared to discuss experience with other healthcare organizations in *detail*. In addition, ask that they provide references. You should make sure that they provide references that are as similar to you as possible. Ensure that the vendor has experience in delivering the services aspect of the work for implementation, or that they partner with an organization that has experience with services.

- **Make the reference calls.** Keep in mind that the vendors gave you these people because they are confident that they will get a good reference. But the information is still valuable. Ask the references questions about deployment, what hiccups they had, anything that the vendors represented as easy or done that wasn't. Ask about the services organization they worked with and how they did their work. Finally, ask them if they would do it again and if so what if anything they would change. If they wouldn't do it again ask them why not.

- **Narrow it down.** Invite the finalists (preferably just two) back to do an in-depth half day with your IT team. Ask about things like total cost of ownership and administration of the product. Ask about security administration and ease of use, particularly with reporting and audit controls for security. That will come in handy if you ever need to determine who had access to what data and for how long. Ask them to bring along their best offer pricing. You will need to know how many licenses you will need and what types of users you will have. If you are doing a mobile deployment you will need to know numbers for that as well.

- **Discuss the details.** Contracting is the least fun part of this process. Keep in mind that even though you ask for their best offer pricing you will still have room to negotiate.

That may mean negotiating on things like length of time for discount (vendors are unlikely to go beyond 18 months, but one year is standard), to assistance with training and deployment. Remember that licenses and services are different so factor that into the pricing. Most vendors can't move on maintenance fees, so don't waste too much time trying to squeeze them on that.

- **Make a "no regrets" decision.** Bring the steering committee together and review all the information together. Agree as a committee to make a no-regrets decision to move forward with one of the vendors. The cost of waiting on the decision is too great to not just move forward.

Regardless of the method, traditional RFP or basic due diligence will likely bring you to a conclusion that your organization can live with. The process for determining which method is right for you has a lot to do with how your organization buys things. If you know that your organization will require a formal RFP process, follow these steps to get the best result for the effort. Most of the mainstream BI tools can do what needs to be done. Make your decision and move on to the real work.

How to Save Time

Finally, when we talk about repeatability, one of the biggest time and energy savers is information architecture. Specifically, when we apply the business rules to the data, we consistently get the same information in our data warehouse. That means that we only have to define it once and create a business rule for it once. We can reuse the information thousands of times in different analyses, dashboards, or reports, but we only had to apply the definition and business rule once.

Definition

Data integrity is applying standards, both data quality and definitions, to data for completeness and consistency.

Not only is this a big time-saver but it's also a big data integrity saver. For many organizations that I work with today, what I find is a team of analysts running queries, lots and lots of queries. When I ask them where they find the definition for the values that they are creating, in other words, how do they define a *patient*, they answer based on their own knowledge. Then I go to the next analyst and ask them how they define a patient, and I get a completely different answer based on their knowledge. This is why you can ask one question and get many different answers. As an organization you have to define and commit to one definition of your data, and apply these business rules in your BI program to ensure that everyone who uses it is using the same data. This is what is often referred to as "one version of the truth." For more on data quality, refer to Chapter 3.

Flexibility

Definition

Flexibility requires all aspects of the architectural structure to flex allowing for changes, edits, and growth within the system while still meeting the nonfunctional requirements associated with performance, security, and availability of the system.

In engineering it is a well-known fact that things that are rigid are weaker. This reminds me of a story my brother told about the first time he ever flew in a large airplane. He was seated in a window seat over the wing. After takeoff he looked out and noticed that the wing was moving quite noticeably up and down. He stopped the flight attendant and asked her if that was normal. Indeed, she said it was, and then he quickly shut the shade and asked for a drink.

The strength of our data warehouses rely on their flexibility. In Table 5.1 I outline the aspects of architecture that are most relevant to each category, but the truth is, for flexibility, it's vital that we consider flexibility in every aspect of the design. I lightheartedly refer to this as *Semper Gumby*, always flexible.

Always Flexible

Certainly there is a big part of platform architecture that must remain flexible. Despite our best attempts, it's completely possible that we may need to add hardware as data and end-user demand increases. If we design our platform to scale appropriately, that means we allow for the flexibility to add servers to meet demand. In today's world that requires that we have the physical space to keep these machines. But the future is now and cloud technologies, or *the cloud* may be a better resolution to our growing hardware infrastructure needs. The decision of whether you keep your hardware in-house is one that many healthcare organizations have and will struggle with. It does allow for flexibility without much more than a signature on a purchase order. In Chapter 8 we discuss the good and bad about the cloud.

Our Hero: Solution Architecture

A few months ago I finally broke down and replaced my dumb phone with a smart phone. I had a BlackBerry a few years before and the experience was less than positive. I was hesitant to give up my simple and easy-to-use phone for another too-smart phone. Certainly, it was a hassle to carry a music player, GPS, tablet, and my dumb phone, but they all were simple devices that did their jobs and didn't cause me grief. Until the day my phone battery wouldn't hold a charge and I knew that the inevitable day was upon me.

My experience with the phone is similar to that experience of software users. They know that there is something out there that can meet their needs better, but change is too hard. Users are a fickle bunch. They are quick to complain about the software they use to do a task, but when you try to replace it with something new that meets their needs better, they are quick to complain about that, too. However, if you stick with outdated and antiquated software, you violate many of the abilities we have outlined in this chapter.

Solution architecture may well be the unsung hero of BI programs. This level of architecture is where you integrate your transactional systems, it's where application architecture "lives," and it most closely reflects the business and operational processes of the organization to ensure that all solutions meet the business needs. That leaves a lot of balls for a solution architect to juggle.

The Art of Data

The ability to design a data architecture that can grow over time with minimal impact is an art form. Terms exist that attempt to cover the topic, such as *open architecture* or *service-oriented architecture*. Both terms were defined in the context of the information technology industry and adapted for data warehousing. The importance of these or any definitions is the idea that we create the data structures to support the growth, changes, and updates to our business.

In Chapter 2, I referenced a story about a less-than-optimized data model. Specifically, what we had done was "architected" ourselves into a corner, because when we started we didn't know or understand all of the relationships in the data because they didn't exist yet. Our growth through acquisition had put us behind the eight ball. Each time our business model changed or acquired another business, we should have spent the time to make the appropriate modifications to the data model. That never happened and as a result we had a catastrophic failure of the function.

Data models can be built to be flexible, but they can't be built to be psychic. When your business model goes through a significant change (e.g., accountable care organizations) take the time to modify the data model. It's the most valuable commitment you can make to your BI program.

For you business leaders, I hope that these pages have brought some clarity to the complex and confusing world of BI architecture. I wish that there were a silver bullet that could address all of the layers of architecture that organizations have to address to build a BI program, but there isn't. The closest any of us can get to a silver bullet is a great partner who has enough IT experience to guide and deliver the architectural aspects of BI.

Notes

Hughes, R. (2008). *Agile Data Warehousing: Delivering World Class Business Intelligence Systems using Scrum and XP*. Bloomington: iUniverse.

Madsen, L., and R. Nemani (2011, April 27). *ETL for Healthcare Business Intelligence*. Retrieved December 12, 2011, from BeyeNetwork.com: http://www.b-eye-network.com/view/15148.

Mattran, R. (2006). *The Five Disciplines of Business Intelligence*. Minneapolis.

TechTarget. (2000, September). *SearchDataCenter.com*. Retrieved December 2011, from SearchDataCenter.com: http://searchdatacenter.techtarget.com/definition/scalability.

Wikipedia. (2010, May). Wikipedia. Retrieved December 19, 2011, from Usability: http://en.wikipedia.org/wiki/Usability.

CHAPTER 6

Providing Value

Whoever said "perception is reality" knew a thing or two about business intelligence (BI) programs. This is one of the most challenging tenets to address; the reasons for this are numerous. First and foremost, management of many BI programs still resides within an IT function. Some IT groups are very adept at providing content, releases, the latest "thing," but providing business value requires a new level of participation by the business, which is why sponsorship is so important to BI programs. Another challenge to providing value is the shifting tides of business users. If I had a dime for every time I heard an IT person say about a business user "They just don't know what they want," I would be a thousandaire. I promise you, businesspeople know exactly what they want; they can't articulate it in words that most IT people understand. The shifting tides of business users are usually shifting because that is the nature of the business. Healthcare has never been so radically changed as it has been in the past two years in the United States. It's tough to prioritize when everything is important and regulated. Therefore, it is our job as BI professionals to find ways to deliver value as quickly as possible.

Value, at the end of the day, is what our end-users perceive it to be. If we make their lives easier by providing the right information at the right time in the right way, that is value. The devil, of course, is in the details.

In this chapter we cover the methods of increasing value. We include some tried-and-true methods that bring great value to the BI program over time, such as increasing user adoption and learning about a health system that took the value of their data to a new level. Sometimes providing value is just a matter of letting people know what you are doing, so we discuss how to market your BI program. But first, we have to create a team that delivers value. So we discuss the BI team, roles and responsibilities, and where BI sits in the organizational structure.

Creating a BI Team

A little bit of magic happens when a great team is created. The synergy, creativity, and satisfaction drive innovative thinking and tangible results. But getting there can be a real challenge. BI teams are no different, and the pressures on them today can make it even more difficult to create a solid base from which to work. However, it is important that we structure our teams so they are in the best position for success.

Before we get into the specifics about how the team is structured, we need to address where the BI team resides within the organization. I have a strong opinion about this because I have only seen BI teams succeed when a certain set of key factors exist. The BI team needs to reside in the business side of the organization. I know that many of you are likely stating your arguments to the contrary right now. Believe me, I have heard them. If you review all of the previous chapters, covering the tenets of healthcare BI, what you will find consistently is the integration of business. The team needs to be well-aligned to the IT function that will support them. IT is critically important to the BI function, but it cannot drive the bus. Business intelligence is about the business, and therefore must be led by the business.

Your BI leader, report developers, data governance, and report consultants should all reside on the BI team. The folks with more technical skills (such as the extract, transform, and load [ETL] developers and architects) should stay in IT. Of the utmost importance is the alignment between IT and the business. Any disconnect here allows for misaligned incentives and increases the likelihood of failure. Even if your BI leader and IM (information management) leader are assigned organizational accountability to two different entities, such as the CIO (chief information officer) and executive sponsor, that's better than having the first organizational connection at the CEO level.

The Healthcare BI Team

I have heard good BI skill sets described a number of different ways. One version is the "T" people, who have some breadth of knowledge but usually a lot of depth in one area. Alternatively, the "Purple People," who have a combination of business, referred to as "Blue People," and the IT skill set, referred to as "Red People"; mix them together and you get purple. Both of these types of descriptions are trying to articulate that BI professionals are horses of a different color. They are neither exclusively business-focused nor IT professionals. If you look at their background you are likely to find training in one and a significant amount of experience in another.

I like extending the T people to a team, so that you have a group of people with a fair amount of breadth and a group of people with a lot of depth. That's all good, but you can't put in a job description, "We are looking for purple people with T tendencies." When hiring in the past I have looked for those people who get bored easily. It's usually not a personality trait most hiring managers look for, but in BI it's critical, because BI is so multifaceted and diverse. One minute I will be talking with an executive about metrics that drive the business, and the next minute I will be talking with my DBA (database administrator) about indexing tables to improve performance. It's difficult to get bored easily when so much intellectual stimulation is going on. But that only works for people who seek that level of stimulation. For those who prefer the quieter side, they will find BI too tangential and distracting.

Perhaps the most significant challenge is actually finding the right type of resource with knowledge in the healthcare industry and the specific toolsets that your organization uses. Thankfully, BI as a skill set has grown tremendously over the past few years, but it is still really hard to find a resource with much healthcare industry experience; even more difficult is to find a good BI leader with industry experience. Start your search early, and be prepared to relocate people or be willing to compromise on what skill sets are most important. I have worked with a broad array of BI professionals; Table 6.1 shows an outline of the type of person who suits the role well.

The roles outlined in Figure 6.1 are the primary ones that support a BI program. You may not need all of these, or you may already have some of these people on staff. Some roles can be combined with others (such as ETL architect and developer), but others should be exclusive. It's also important to note that you don't need all of these roles the first day you start your BI initiative.

The BI developer role is integral to the success of any BI team. The BI developer role is the bread and butter of the BI team. These developers are responsible for the creation of reports and dashboards. Not everyone can do this job well. First, you have to find someone with deep knowledge of the tool or tools that your organization uses. In some roles the technology depth is not required, but for BI developers that isn't the case. They have to know the tool and know it well. Second is their ability to communicate; the closer I can put that developer to the user the better the result, so I want someone who can explain

TABLE 6.1 Business Intelligence Organizational Chart

Title	Role and Description	Reporting Structure
Director, BI	Responsible for the vision of BI for the organization and accountable for the successful deployment of BI.	Reports up through the business, preferably the executive sponsor (e.g., CFO)
BI Architect	Responsible for technical communication between IT and BI teams, accountable for the overall architecture of the BI platform. This role requires a technical skillset.	Reports to BI leader
ETL Architect	Responsible for the design of a ETL and the application of best practices.	Reports to the IT organization
BI Developer	Responsible for the development of reports and dashboards.	Reports up through the BI leader, could report to the BI architect if needed
ETL Developer	Responsible for the application of business rules and data quality standards into the transformation scripts that loads the data warehouse.	Reports through the IT organization
Report Consultants	Responsible for customer service associated with your BI program. Consider requiring this role to have some clinical expertise, particularly if you are in a provider organization that will help customer service to the clinical staff.	Reports to BI leader

(continued)

TABLE 6.1 (*Continued*)

Title	Role and Description	Reporting Structure
Business Analysts	Responsible for documenting business requirements to be passed to the BI developers for creation of reports and dashboards.	Reports to BI leader
Quality Analyst	Responsible for the analysis of data in the data warehouse to ensure data is certified. This role is optional, particularly if you have a highly engaged business organization that will fill this role.	Reports to the IT organization
Information Architect	Responsible for the architectural aspects of the data warehouse. Must have a strong partnership with the BI architect, sometimes they can be one and the same.	Reports to the IT organization

things in accessible terms, not tech talk. Finally, and perhaps the most challenging to measure, is the ability to be innovative and flexible. Sometimes highly technical people can't see beyond what the technology can and can't do. I don't want that limited vision in a developer. I need someone who solves problems, not creates them.

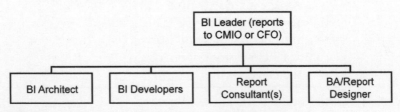

FIGURE 6.1 Business Intelligence Organizational Chart

Closely related to the BI developer is the ETL developer. I need these folks to be strong in technology and creative— problem-solving thinkers. The ETL developer applies the business rules into scripts that transform the data and loads it into the data warehouse. The ability to communicate is less critical with these roles because it will be a rare instance (although it does happen) where I will put them in touch with my end-user. When this does happen, I generally have someone join the conversation, such as a BI architect or a data analyst.

The BI architects are the heart of not only your team but the program as a whole. They need to have lots of experience and knowledge in a variety of toolsets. Their communication skills have to be top-notch because they will be working with the end-users as well as directors and executives throughout the organization. Creativity is critical in their line of work, and you find that many good architects make drawings to get their point across.

Report consultants are a resource type that I don't see much in my travels through healthcare organizations. They usually have someone filling this role but they don't call them report consultants. I did this job early in my career, and it is good experience for those folks starting out. I create these roles to be the first responders to calls or emails with questions about the reports. In one organization, there was a team of four registered nurses (RNs) who were called *liaisons*. That level of expertise isn't always required; it depends on what you are reporting on. But what is required is someone with an excellent communication style who works well under pressure and can handle 20 calls a day on questions like "How do I reset my password?" and "How come that window pops up when I move my mouse?" (i.e., "tooltip").

I frequently get asked, "Who should be on my BI team?" and I often answer with something like: "You will need a BI report developer, a couple of ETL developers, a BI architect, a few report consultants (folks that serve your end customer), and a BI leader." And that's all true, varying slightly on how large your budget and organization is. But what I have come to realize is that people generally aren't asking me about roles, but about what *types of people* should fill these roles.

Example: Director, Business Intelligence Job Description

Position Summary Business intelligence is an interactive process for exploring and analyzing structured, domain-specific information (often stored in data warehouses) to discern business trends or patterns thereby deriving insights and drawing conclusions. The business intelligence process includes communicating findings and effecting change across the organization.

The director of business intelligence is responsible for creation and support of an enterprise business intelligence program and management of the data warehouse for business use. This includes, but is not limited to, information governance, requirements gathering, report development, support of end-users, management of the data assets, generating demand for usage of data, and creating an effective communication and marketing plan for the enterprise data warehouse.

Responsibilities:

- Owns or directly shapes the BI strategy, architecture, and budget
- Facilitates the prioritization of projects and requirements among competing business interests

- Oversees the program, project managers, architects, and specialists
- Establishes standards for technology and business processes
- Coordinates and aligns multiple data warehousing projects
- Meets business criteria for successful BI implementations
- Interfaces with business sponsors and steering committees

Qualifications:

- Ten years' experience in business intelligence and data warehousing
- Knowledge of key tools such as Oracle, SQL Server, MicroStrategy, and SAS
- Current knowledge of the data warehouse market, vendors, and standards bodies
- Demonstrated skills in critical decision making under pressure are required
- Excellent verbal and written communication skills required. Communication to teams must provide clarity and drive toward implementation
- Versed in best software development practices and demonstrated ability to propagate this knowledge to development resources

When I think of each of these roles I see the faces of the people I have worked with over the years who are the perfect fit for the role—my friend Rao, who is the best ETL developer I have ever known; Jonathan, an architect in every sense of the word; a whole team of creative developers who would tell me

I was asking for the impossible and deliver it anyway. So when I consider how to create an incredible BI team, I know that finding the right people is the key and that means a fair amount of art and luck are involved.

As you begin, determine the level of expertise you need for each role. Technical prowess, healthcare knowledge, communication skills, and innovation are always my top four. It's also important to consider a good organizational fit. If you have a traditional, hierarchal organization, then avoid the "maverick" report developer who thinks standards are for wimps. If you have a small organization where everyone wears multiple hats, avoid the people who have honed their skills at a large organization where keeping within the confines of your job grade is rewarded. For those roles on the "softer" side of BI, such as data governance and "report consultants," my preference is for excellent communication skills and the ability to navigate politically charged situations with charm and grace. I can teach them the ins and outs of BI; it's harder to teach someone how to respond in a highly emotional situation.

User Adoption

Now that we have a team structure that is set up for success, we have to focus on how we deliver the capabilities to our users. User adoption is the life-blood of the BI organization. Without it BI will not survive. Users can make or break your program, so we give a lot of thought as to how to best support them. Healthcare will always require a value-driven investment strategy. If you can provide a BI program that supports all the different types of healthcare business users, then the value will be created by those users and the investment will be an easy and obvious one. Certainly, good BI can be business transformative, but bad BI is just plain expensive.

The ability to demonstrate value in a quantifiable form comes down to three letters: ROI, return on investment. If you have many users on your system, the investment is generally considered a good one. But volume doesn't always mean value, and your leadership may ask you to look beyond user numbers and report numbers and determine the ROI of your BI program. The good news is that all it takes is one user making a big discovery that saves the company money. That could be found in process improvement, product development, or just operational efficiency. But users are fickle, and big blockbuster discoveries aren't common. ROI demonstrates value but doesn't create value. That is why the actual method of doing an ROI analysis is covered in Chapter 4.

First we need to establish a common framework in which to discuss user adoption. Next, we discuss the recommended steps to create good adoption and the tools needed to get started on your user adoption program. Finally, a section is dedicated to the measurement of your user adoption program.

The trinity of user adoption provides you with your framework (see Figure 6.2). All the steps for increasing user adoption

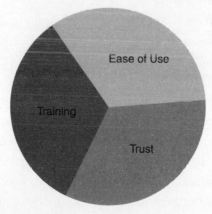

FIGURE 6.2 The Trinity of User Adoption

directly address one of these three concepts. Although you may feel strongly about one over another, these three work in harmony. Without one, the others are not strong enough on their own to hold up user adoption.

Ease of Use and the Google Effect

First, we need to understand the impact that the general user interface (GUI) has had on user adoption. In the past 10 years, Google has changed the way we look at the GUI. Nothing so simple yet effective has been produced before or since. Google makes it so simple to enter a search term and get 12,200,200 results back in .12 seconds. This alone has radically changed the way everyone interacts with software. I call this "the Google effect" and it impacts almost all areas of BI user adoption because it fosters expectations about *simplicity* and *performance*, two things that every BI practitioner should take notice of.

Users have become much more sophisticated, but they also expect simplicity. Most BI user interfaces are not particularly elegant. Many of the BI applications have come a long way, but most of them still have a lot of functionality on the primary landing page. BI tools are not search engines, and their interface will never be that simple. But we need to consider the design and development from a user experience perspective. Simplicity can be measured by counting the clicks. Research varies on how many clicks are too many, but the average user seems to get frustrated by about the 10th click.

The other impact from Google is performance. User interface aside, the real challenge is duplicating the performance that users experience with Google. A user once asked me, "If I can get 14,000,000 results back in less than a second in Google why can't my two-page report return in less than five minutes?" She was frustrated, and my inclination was to sit her down and draw on a whiteboard the difference between a healthcare multidimensional model, aggregation of data, and so on, versus Google pulling 14,000,000 results for "Chicken Recipe." I decided against the lecture. Truth be told, we have made incredible strides in performance. When I started all reports ran overnight and delivered the next day. But we aren't Google and we may never have that level of performance consistently.

Improve Training to Reduce the Effect of Attention Scarcity

Just about every week an article appears on a major news syndicate talking about the impact of our lifestyle, stress, and health. With all the tweeting, Facebooking, texting, emailing, and calling we do, it's amazing that we have any time to stop and concentrate. The attention scarcity that most of us suffer from has a big impact on BI. If some users only run reports quarterly, what are the odds that they can remember everything over a gap or of three months? They cannot remember any nuances associated with running reports, so your first line of defense is to *ban all nuances*. Make report running as clean as possible.

Attention scarcity highlights the need for training and user support within a BI program. A few years ago I was at a company that had a BI tool with little adoption and lots of complaints. People asked me, "Is the tool bad?" After having a couple conversations, I realized that no one was responsible for the tool. No one was managing what went in, what came out, and how to address user concerns. Users were ignored, written off as difficult, or told that there were no resources to accommodate the request. The tool wasn't bad, their process was. They had no user support. This isn't the *Field of Dreams*—if you build it,

147

you've only done about 40 percent of the work, and users will not necessarily come.

Managing Expectations to Build Trust

One theory in psychology postulates that the larger the gap between a person's perception and reality, the more likely that individual will be depressed. That theory also applies to the usage of a BI tool. If expectations aren't met, there will be dissatisfaction among the ranks.

Expectation management is the key. The BI tool is just a tool—it is not Nirvana. It will not make you smarter, faster, or thinner. You must build the trust of the user base from early on by tailoring your communications. As you communicate, keep in mind that trust is a result of four factors:

1. **Accessibility:** Let's face it—if the software or the data is not accessible, not much else matters. Luckily, accessibility is not usually a big problem. But if you know that your ETL process is performance-challenged, or lacks the appropriate frequency, then you need to address the issue.
2. **Reliability:** This means that users can trust that the results will be accurate and dependable, over and over again, no matter how or when they access the data.
3. **Consistency:** If one thing can drive a data person crazy, it's different results for no "good" reason. If the same query is run twice, the results had better be the same. Nothing deteriorates trust quicker than a well-informed and *vocal* power user.
4. **Honesty:** Billy Joel probably said it best: "*Honesty is hardly ever heard, and mostly what I need from you.*" No one likes to confess that during the data load someone accidentally dropped a table (true story), or that some of the code was inadvertently dropping records that ended with a "1" (also

a true story). Maybe you don't need to tell users the gory details, but you need to tell them enough so they understand any delay or change in the data. You need to be timely and forthright. They will know when you are dishonest and it will degrade trust.

The BI User Persona Continuum

Not all BI users are created equal. I learned this the hard way when I was busy implementing a new BI tool. We had a strong ROI and were writing an add-on to provide additional capability. Early in the project I spoke with other users, but as development ramped up I served as the primary designer and tester. When the add-on was released, all hell broke loose. About 80 percent of our user base complained that it was "clunky" and "difficult to use." At first, I chalked it up to fear of change. But after a while I noticed something: the analysts weren't complaining about the add-on. As a matter of fact they had no issues with it whatsoever.

I had developed a concept of a user continuum early in my career, but as a result of this experience, I was able to formalize my theory of the continuum and the two persona types at each end.

The Executive Persona

In Figure 6.3, the left side of the spectrum represents the executive user who doesn't have time to learn any subtleties. These individuals need a simple user interface, and when possible, an immediate response to a query. A good example is a CEO who ideally comes into work in the morning, turns on the computer, and sees a dashboard with all the key operating metrics. If the metrics are all green, then all is well. If anything appears in red, then some phone calls are urgently needed.

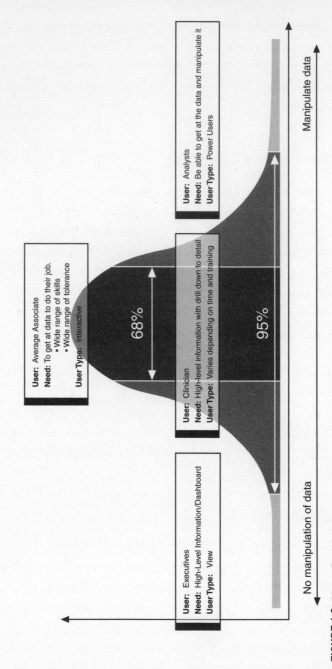

User: Average Associate
Need: To get at data to do their job.
• Wide range of skills
• Wide range of tolerance
User Type: Interactive

User: Analysts
Need: Be able to get at the data and manipulate it
User Type: Power Users

User: Clinician
Need: High-level information with drill down to detail
User Type: Varies depending on time and training

User: Executives
Need: High-Level Information/Dashboard
User Type: View

68%

95%

No manipulation of data

Manipulate data

FIGURE 6.3 User Continuum

The executive is rare, but the term doesn't always imply a senior level of management. The executive is just a person who doesn't have much time or capability to respond to prompts.

The Analyst Persona

On the far right side of the continuum are the analysts. Today, most organizations have many analysts, in title anyway. I am referring to the people who know the data intimately, the true "power users." They are the people you go to when you need answers. As a generalization, analysts prefer to get their hands right into the data. They don't mind a less-than-friendly user interface; they focus on the end result much more than the journey. For most organizations the true analysts are less than 3 percent of the staff.

The Clinical Persona

Clinicians are a tricky breed when it comes to BI. They are incredibly sophisticated consumers of research, statistics, and data. Most of them have spent the past decade reading research articles. But once they get into practice, the pressures of seeing patients as quickly as possible means that their time is precious. Therefore, you have a bimodal distribution; this simply means that clinicians are like executives and analysts all in one. They have the ability to consume very detailed and sophisticated data analyses, but they just don't have the time.

The Average Associate Persona

The majority of your users fall into the middle of the bell curve, they vary in their skill sets and capabilities. Where some are just barely able to respond to prompts, others will border on being analysts. The majority of this group has the ability to respond to prompts and run basic reports without much trouble. Because of their varying skill level, the "Interactive" users are the most difficult to manage. For example, something like a clunky add-on wouldn't faze the users toward the right side of the middle; the ones toward the left side almost have nervous breakdowns.

Six Steps to Providing Value

Now that we understand the framework of user adoption, and we have identified the major groups of end-users we will be delivering to, we can explore the six steps to increased user adoption.

Step 1: Know Your Users by Creating Personas

Ideally, you would use personas to help target your development and communications. A number of methods can be used to create these personas. The most practical is to create a survey that will help generate the distribution of user types. As we discussed earlier there are generally four user types in a healthcare organization (see Figure 6.3), but you might be different and have three or five. Your first step is to determine the distribution by listing all your users (if you have thousands, then take a random sample) and place them into the four categories (more or fewer as needed).

SURVEY SAYS   If you don't know your users that well or have too many users to create a good baseline, then you can create a simple survey. Keep the survey short. You want as many of your users to complete it as possible. The questions should be focused on the user preference, flexibility, and capability.

Here are some sample questions:

1. How comfortable are you with using [BI Tool name]?
   - ☐ I am very comfortable (1)
   - ☐ I am comfortable (2)
   - ☐ I am fairly comfortable (3)
   - ☐ I am not very comfortable (4)
   - ☐ I not comfortable (5)
2. Do people usually ask for your help when they use [BI Tool name]?
   - ☐ Yes (1)
   - ☐ No (2)
3. How would you rate your knowledge of the data?
   - ☐ Expert (1)
   - ☐ Fairly knowledgeable (2)
   - ☐ Knowledgeable (3)
   - ☐ Less knowledgeable (4)
   - ☐ Not at all knowledgeable (5)
4. What do you do when a report returns a result you didn't expect (e.g., returns a higher member count than you anticipated)?
   - ☐ Ask a colleague for assistance (4)
   - ☐ Recheck my parameters (3)
   - ☐ Rerun the report (2)
   - ☐ Run a separate query using a different tool (1)
   - ☐ Other, describe

Keep in mind that this is self-reporting, so some people may assume they know more than they really do. But for the most part, that shouldn't throw off your curve. These questions are not exhaustive, so you should create some that are specific to your environment and situation. The scoring methodology for these reports will help you create your distribution. Run a frequency distribution for each of these questions. The frequency of the lower scores (one and two) means that you have more of the analyst persona, the frequency of the middle score denotes the average associate persona, and if you have many high scores, that indicates a high number of the executive persona (remember that you don't have to be an executive to meet the executive persona type).

Once your distribution is complete, you can understand the dynamics of your user base. If you have many executives, you know you have to focus on a simplified user interface and performance. Your development efforts should be aimed toward dashboards and scorecards rather than standard reports. Your program's support structure should be highly streamlined. If at all possible, the executive user should have one person to call to resolve or report issues.

The analyst persona doesn't require as much hand-holding, but data quality is paramount. Data quality is important for all user types, but power users tend to be in the detail data and the differences between aggregated and detail data can sometimes be a challenge. Another consideration for the power user types is documentation. They will be less likely to attend additional training sessions, preferring to work their way through it. But they will refer to available documentation, so as much detail as possible should go into the documentation provided to them.

If your program is like many others and you find yourself with a middle majority of "interactive" users, you have your work cut out for you. You will have to address the aspects of both the executive and analyst persona in this one user type. As you consider the continuum, you will see that some of these users are like analysts and some are like executives; the rest fall into a category of their own. For the most part, your average associate users will be the easiest group to manage. They will easily respond to prompts, regularly run reports, and attend training updates. But regardless of user type, users don't like a lot of change. Anything that changes how they interact with the tool, even if it's an improvement, can really throw them off.

When changes happen, and they will, you must prepare them early and often. Try to be as concrete with your examples as possible and give them "sneak peeks" of the development. If it's an upgrade to a newer release, have your vendor come in, give a preview, and answer questions. Post the release notes in a shared location so everyone knows what will happen. Post the high-level project plan so everyone knows the schedule, too.

FOR THOSE JUST STARTING   If you are just starting your BI program and haven't selected a tool yet, it's still a good idea to create a persona survey and distribute. This will help inform your tool selection process. Once you have completed the persona work, it is time to start the selection process. Your first step is to determine the features that users want.

Remember to select the tool based on your users and their needs and preferences, not based on tool features, because that can turn your typical request for proposal (RFP) BI tool selection process on its head (see Chapter 5 for more information on the RFP process). There was a time when the best practice was to gather requirements from your business—a great first step, unless your business was uninformed about what was possible. Those requirements were then documented and prioritized, and the vendors would be scored against the requirements. The requirements would often read something like, "The BI tool must be user friendly." But what does that really mean? For each user the definition of "user friendly" could vary (and does vary) drastically, as we learned from our persona analysis. Perhaps the BI tool can do all kinds of great things, but if your users will never use those "features," it doesn't matter. It reminds me of the adage in software development: There is no such thing as a bug, only a "feature." Just because a product can do something doesn't mean it provides value.

Ideally, before selecting a tool, spend some time understanding your user's wants, needs, and capabilities. You will be creating personas of users, so you will be able to validate the tools capabilities against the base persona for a standard user. Take the time to understand what *user friendly* means to the executives, nurse managers, and analysts. When vendors come in to pitch their products, let these user types determine how user-friendly the tool is out of the box. You can customize any BI tool to improve the user-friendliness, and that may be necessary at some point, but you want to assess the out-of-the-box capabilities so you know how quickly the tool will be providing value. With all the work to do when first bringing on a BI tool, you don't want to have to spend as much time prettying up the GUI as you do preparing the data for consumption.

Step 2: Fixing Your User Interface

You know something has really caught on when we have made it a verb. Google™ has become so ubiquitous that we take it for granted, but BI practitioners can learn a lot from Google. First, its home page is sparse, even though they could have sold that real estate for a lot of money. They understood early on that you have to put what users want up front. This concept has yet to find its way into our user interfaces. After log in, most tools expect you to know where you are going and why. The folder structures are left up to the administrators and I have seen folder structures more than 13 layers deep. The user would have to click more than 10 times just to find the screen they need. Some users are better than others at understanding the concept of categories of reports (linking like reports into a category to reduce the need to dig through folders), but it still requires a folder structure as its primary location.

COUNT THE CLICKS Try this experiment. Log into your BI tool and count every click it takes to run a report and return. If you click less than 10 times, you are doing well. If more than 10, look for opportunities to streamline the structure. Is it possible to completely revamp your folder structure? Can you use the customizable aspect of your tool to have users place their frequently run reports in a personal folder or location? Keep in mind that this will only get you part of the way there. Don't worry about the users who are familiar with the system; it's the rest of the users who will benefit most from a streamlining exercise.

Take every opportunity to clean up your user interface. Put frequently run reports high in the report structure. Use a basic color scheme with very little extra stuff. Where it is possible and necessary, guide the users through certain aspects of the system (such as a wizard capability for ad hoc usage). It is helpful to put the content into the conceptual framework of the tools that users know best, such as Microsoft™ Excel to help them quickly adjust to using new tools. That may seem counterintuitive to most BI practitioners, preferring to keep the users in the system they have the most control over, but in the words of UI designer Joel Spolsky:

> *The point is, does the user interface (UI) respond to the user in the way in which the user expected it to respond? If it didn't, the user is going to feel helpless and out of control.*
> **Controlling Your Environment Makes You Happy, April 10, 2000.** (www.joelonsoftware.com/uibook/chapters/fog0000000057.html)

Step 3: Address Performance

I dream of a day when the business intelligence and data warehouse industry is able to return millions of rows of data in .7 seconds, like Google can. Until then we'll have to do our best to make the user experience as efficient as possible. Performance is almost never a BI tool issue (notice I did say "almost never"—a few memory hogs are out there with a lot of overhead). For the most part, this is where the real magic happens. A good data model with a solid infrastructure should return most query requests in a minute or less. If yours doesn't, then it may be time to assess the issues that are impacting performance. It's best to first consider the "usual suspects" when it comes to performance degradation. Certainly taking a look at how your hardware is configured is an easy first step. Once you clear that hurdle you could consider the speed of Internet connections. These vary a great deal, and if your users are on a slow line your hands are tied in your ability to address it, but verifying it can be a small victory. Finally, you may want to reconsider how your data is structured. I talk quite a bit about the architecture in Chapter 5, and I won't repeat myself here, but performance is important to the long-term success so leave no stone unturned.

Step 4: Metadata Is Mandatory

Communication is the key principle in engaging users. We have to provide many different types of communication to ensure an engaged user base, and we will be responsible for the communication throughout the life span of a BI program. One of the longest standing and important ones to user adoption is metadata. Simply, metadata is the agreed on business definition of the data. It is necessary to invest the time and energy in creating and maintaining metadata because it is the primary way that end-users learn what the data represents. It's not necessarily the first thing that you build, but it must be built.

Many of the popular BI tools have some mechanism for managing metadata. Some have separate products that address the need. Consider the metadata manager that comes with your

BI tool because it will simplify the creation and management of metadata. With that said, as long as you have a shared location and a document that cannot be updated by just anyone, then you have the basics of what you need. The latter option will take many more resources to manage, but metadata helps broaden user adoption by giving people a mechanism to learn about the data being reported. If metadata is missing, they will often question results and find back doors to validate results unnecessarily.

Step 5: Always Teaching: Your Path to an Enlightened End-User Community

I have had four years of French. I have been certified in two BI products. I can neither speak French nor develop reports. The reason is simple: If you don't use it, you lose it. Most users aren't on the system often. They have to do monthly or quarterly reporting. With all of the other responsibilities that the average person has in a day, it's no wonder that people forget how to use something after a month or two. Earlier in this chapter we discussed attention scarcity. As a result I recommended that you nix anything that looks like a nuance when it comes to running reports. I know that's not always possible, but you should strive hard during your development phase to avoid the reflex of saying, "That's a training issue." There will indeed be some, but they should be the exception not the rule. Things that become training issues become questions from end-users, or assumptions by end-users. Training issues can take up a lot of time from your report consultants, and may produce poor results if this one-off isn't documented and well-communicated to *every* user that it may impact. Any inconsistency can degrade the trust of the business users; therefore, "training issues" should be reduced as much as possible.

Think about the 401(k) website that you log into. Odds are you don't log in that often, maybe monthly, maybe annually. You may need a password reminder. But if the website is well designed, that's all you need. If you look closely, you will see no nuances or training issues. These websites are reporting data, too, so we can learn a lot by noticing how easy they make it for us users.

In our BI deployments we must find a way to ensure that our systems are intuitive and easy to navigate. But it's not always possible, so you have to ensure that end-users have the ability to get refreshers. Use your persona development for this work. Each level of your user groups will have different training preferences. Unfortunately, you will have to address them all, because you will have to deliver training to all of your end-users. But knowing what types of end-users you have will help determine what types of training you build out.

Thankfully, today many types of training exist that can fill the need. I would recommend that at a minimum you plan to provide some perpetual computer-based training modules addressing the frequently asked questions (such as "How do I log-in?" or "How do I change the date parameters?"). These modules should be embedded in the landing page or your BI tool, or within a broader portal maintained by your organization. It's imperative to keep these up-to-date. You don't want these modules to represent the log-in page from two years ago if it has radically changed, even if it's just the colors of the page. Users can be quite literal, so make sure that as you update your BI product you update all the CBT modules that are available to end-users. The CBT modules can support many of your basic end-user needs. This will support your beginning end-users and, if built well, can support many of your executive, clinical, average associate, and analyst personas.

Another method that will help with user adoption is to provide some in-person training for the weeks following deployment of anything new. In-person training is expensive and challenging to deploy if you have a geographically dispersed user base. However, it's effective at training end-users for some of the more complex activities such as some ad hoc analysis. As you build this out, make sure that you use your own data and your own screens for this type of training. When training users on the ad hoc environment, those users are typically on the power user end of your continuum, which means that when it comes to data you can't get anything by them. Don't try, either—it will be distracting to them and may impact their perception of the system. It's also a good idea to provide some detailed release notes for reports or your ad hoc environment for your power users.

Somewhere in between the CBT modules and the in-person training will be the rest of your training program. It's essential to note that many different learning styles exist within your user base, and with attention scarcity being prevalent, you will have to work hard to ensure that end-users have all the resources they need at their fingertips to ensure adoption. You can build out distance learning where web-cams are used; you can deliver special training via the portal for certain capabilities (e.g., how to read a dashboard). Creativity counts for training, so make sure that you plan on using multichannels and consistently deliver training, regardless of how long your BI program has been up and running.

Not all end-users will first seek training. Many of them will prefer to have someone to call, so you need a team to answer the calls. Some organizations use their IT help desk; other organizations use the report consultants. The goal is to provide a solution in one phone call. Make sure that the people answering the phone know the system and the answers to the frequently asked questions. This will engender happy users because your first-call resolution rate will be very good, and that's something you can track as part of your program evaluation.

Step 6: Communicate, Understand, and Listen

This step is a big one. It's of great consequence to ensure that every person in the organization knows about the BI program and can articulate the ways it brings value. One way that is successful for BI programs is to plan how to market your program. At this point, you may find yourself recoiling with distaste, saying, "Marketing? I didn't sign up to do any marketing!" Well, it may seem outside your scope, but it is essential. I have seen good programs lose funding because they can't communicate, or haven't consistently communicated, the value proposition of the program. The best way to get started is to write a marketing plan. A marketing plan's function is to organize ideas and plan all critical steps.

CREATE A MARKETING PLAN FOR YOUR PROGRAM As a BI insider, you know that your program is valuable, but how do you safeguard it from being cut when the budget gets tight? How do you show everyone the value of investing $5 million to organize all your data? The answer is a strong internal marketing plan that will demonstrate the value to your stakeholders and make them as dedicated to the program as you are.

A good marketing plan will have six main sections:

1. Align with the mission statement of your organization.
2. Write a powerful program objective.
3. Create a communication plan.
4. Identify the competitive landscape.
5. Be creative with marketing activities.
6. Build a project plan.

ALIGNING WITH YOUR ORGANIZATIONAL MISSION STATEMENT First of all, you must align your program with the mission statement of your organization. In fact, the mission statement of your organization should inform your BI program. After all, the BI program was created by the organization to deliver value back to the organization. If your program doesn't represent the organization as a whole then you are handicapped from the start. If you paid someone for a service and didn't receive the service, you would write that person off forever. Your organization is paying for this service, so make sure that they get what they are paying for.

All of your objectives should be aligned from the highest level (mission statement) to the lowest level (data warehouse content). The reverse is true, too; as you release content into your data warehouse, the business capabilities should align directly to a mission statement. If your hospital has been focusing on improving the outcomes of your diabetic population, so should your content. For example, if your hospital has improved the A1c rating of your diabetic population, and next it aims to improve the frequency of eye exams, your reports will need to align with that goal.

Example: Sample Mission Statement

The mission statement of My Health System is to improve the health of the people and communities we serve and to manage illness with skill and compassion. To this end, My Health System will provide high-quality healthcare services in a fiscally responsible manner, which contribute to the physical, psychological, social, and spiritual well-being of the patients and community it serves. In addition, My Health System will provide educational and community outreach activities to the community for the promotion of good health.

FIGURE 6.4 Marketing Plan

PROGRAM OBJECTIVE As we move from the mission statement to the program objective, you will see that each section is more refined and specific to the BI program than the previous section, much like a funnel (see Figure 6.4).

As with the mission statement, the program objective is an important communication tool. It should tell the reader who, what, and why. For the broader business and IT team working on an individual project, it's an important tool to understanding the program's overall objective.

Your program objectives should align to one of the key statements, such as "The BI Program of My Health System will demonstrate the management of chronic illnesses through high-value reporting and analytics." You will go further by adding "The BI Program will create a dashboard of the fourteen diseases that My Health System monitors. This dashboard will report the level to which each disease is under control based on evidence-based measurement parameters." The more specific and objective you can be, the better able you are to show that you are succeeding against your goals.

When you communicate about the releases, make sure that the connection between the organizational strategy and your release is crystal clear. Start out by saying, "In support of our strategy, the BI team has created a dashboard that reports each disease we manage and the level to which it is managed. As a result we found that we have some opportunities for improvement in . . . "

COMMUNICATION PLAN   If you do nothing else, create the communication plan. Although you will find value in thinking through the other sections of the plan (to ensure alignment), the communication plan is the primary deliverable. I sometimes use customized communication plans for separate subprojects. For example, I have used a communication plan that is specific to an enterprise reporting application; I have also used one for a data stewardship program. Any time you will be consistently sending messages out to your customer base, you should create a communication plan. Most of the time they are incorporated into the marketing plan, but they can be stand-alone, too.

Make sure that your communications are consistent and have an appropriate frequency. Don't underestimate how long communicating takes. Although it seems like it would take no time to write an email and send it, you need to ensure that the message is right on target. Very smart people sometimes communicate to an audience in a way that completely loses the message. Have your draft email proofread by someone in your corporate communications group or marketing team.

Know your audience, regardless of the content you are communicating. Remember the user continuum and your personas (executive, clinical, average associate, and analyst); you should apply the same rules to communicating to your audience as you do when thinking about training the end-user community.

Obviously, you still need to be careful about how you communicate to an external audience. But knowing your audience at this level of specificity will only help target your communication efforts. If you can't create personas, or don't have time, then just know that you have a variety of people in your audience.

Try to have varying levels of communications from bulleted lists to specific explanations (such as release notes).

COMPETITIVE LANDSCAPE   Improving your competitive advantage is often a key deliverable of BI programs. And even if it isn't a deliverable, it's still a good exercise to review what your competition does in its BI programs. You may be able to adopt some ideas or position yourself to make a competitive difference in the future. If you work in an industry that doesn't have traditional competitors such as government or nonprofits, take this opportunity to write a section about what your industry is doing with BI overall. This can help validate investment decisions.

MARKETING ACTIVITIES   This is the central part of the marketing plan. These activities should vary greatly, from formal training to informal emails. For example, if you have to educate the data stewards on the "The Basics of Data Modeling" you could bring in a trainer. You might also send out a biweekly email called "DM Design Tips." They both meet your objective of educating the data stewards on the basics of data modeling. Include success parameters; for example, being able to list at least five people in attendance for something like a BI Book Club. You should be specific regarding any activity that is tied to a budget. Use your marketing plan as a litmus test for your activities. If the planned marketing activity doesn't meet one of the program objectives, then you shouldn't do it. For example, if you have a program objective to expand knowledge about BI best practices throughout the organization, your marketing activity should be aimed at education. Bring in a speaker or disseminate an article about best practices. Holding a bake sale as an activity will do nothing for your objective.

PLAN THE WORK   Take all of the tasks and put them in a project plan. Schedule them so they aren't all happening at once, and allocate time to do them all (estimate the work and line up the resources). Some should repeat and others will be a one-time communication. Spread the work around. Even though the BI group is responsible for the communication, make sure you get as much help as reasonably possible. If you have a big project, you could spend nearly 40 hours a week just communicating to your user base. Most people don't have that kind of time, so work the plan as much as possible.

Now that you have completed the marketing plan and written a project plan, determine who is going to help deliver the content. If you work for a company with an internal marketing team, you are fortunate and your work is almost done. Regardless of who helps you, the BI team needs to take the lead on the communications, particularly if you are communicating to your customers. If you have a BI team, then set up a BI email box and allow other people to author email. Let go and allow others to communicate as much as they can. It will help you focus on the communications to the executives and customers. If you have others who will be sending out communications, take the time to either create a template or train them. It's tempting to make the assumption that because someone has a lot of experience they know how to communicate to a user base. You know what they say about assuming? As the BI leader you are accountable for the communication, so emphasize your expectations about how to communicate effectively.

UNDERSTANDING YOUR AUDIENCE   Now that you have determined how you are going to communicate and have put a plan together, it's time to think about how you are going to listen. Perhaps you have some plans to have user group meetings. This is a great mechanism for hearing feedback. Smaller meetings lend themselves better to conversation; really large meetings are no more effective than a newsletter at eliciting feedback. In addition, you should consider focus groups and frequent one-on-one conversation with users who represent all of your persona user types. Make sure that you don't always talk to the same people; different people offer different perspectives that are important. To make the most of these sessions, make sure that people know that you will be taking notes and following up with each of them on how their feedback was used to improve the program. When new content or functionality is released based on feedback from a user, include that information in the newsletter or release notes. Public acknowledgment is powerful.

NEW INNOVATIONS   Okay, but what if you are the lucky BI practitioner who has a mature program that is up and running and easily meets all of your operational and service level agreement expectations? You have to remember that a BI program is a living, breathing thing. It exists within your organization's ecosystem, which is constantly changing. So you need to find a way to innovate all the time to ensure that the program stays relevant.

Here are three ideas that provide more value with your existing program.

1. If you have access to a lot of data and you are used to just reporting what *has* happened, that's an easy place to take it to the next level; ramp up your goal by trying to *predict* what will happen.
2. If you only have standard, boring spreadsheet-like reports, try creating visually appealing dashboards.
3. Or, if you are looking for ways to get your user group more involved, extend them a challenge to find the most innovative ways to use the data and give a prize to the winner.

Work hard to ensure that you are always providing value.

EVALUATING THE PROGRAM: HOW DO YOU KNOW YOU'RE SUCCESSFUL?

Your enthusiasm may be at its peak right now and your first inclination is to run out and begin implementing these steps, but you need to do something first. You need to define success. As Stephen Covey wrote in *The 7 Habits of Highly Effective People*, one great habit is to "Begin with the end in mind." What do you want to see when you are done? How will you measure an improvement in user adoption? What do your executives consider success? How can you measure it?

We really need to practice what we preach here. The entire reason that BI programs exist is to measure the success of certain efforts (new product launches, customer focused initiatives, etc.). Yet we often forget to measure our own success in an objective way. It's imperative to consider what value means to you and your leadership. Reporting on those metrics requires that you gather the data to support the metrics. Gathering the data can be done in a number of ways, including creating surveys that measure value, satisfaction, and data integrity or simply measure the number of users accessing the tools. The latter is the least valuable way to measure success, because it doesn't put the value of the usage into context, but it can be informative if you use it with other numbers (such as the total number of possible users).

Each healthcare BI organization will have to determine what is most important. A good place to start may be to review the organizational mission statement. Demonstrate the value that the BI program has provided by measuring it against all of the key statements in the mission statement. You can also report on aspects of user satisfaction with the ease of use, customer satisfaction with the training program, or the percentage of first-call resolution. Provide as much transparency as possible by reporting the level of data quality in a dashboard. Not only will you be able to track how successful the user adoption

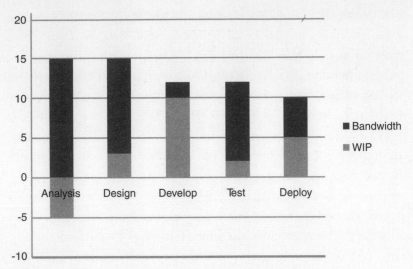

FIGURE 6.5 Communicating Your Development Life Cycle

program is, but these types of reports will also provide transparency and increase trust—thereby improving the value of the program. Provide formal communication to your sponsors, and when communicating to a broader audience, perhaps consider having your executive sponsor contribute to the communication (if only by writing a foreword or sidebar) to showcase executive support (see Figure 6.5).

Evaluation doesn't always have to mean numbers. If someone sends you an email about the great job your team is doing, that is highly valuable qualitative data. Post those statements in a newsletter or on the portal, and once it's possible, categorize them and create a report based on those comments. Another great way to measure success is to find your biggest BI advocates and ask what they are doing with the data. You may learn that they have completed some analysis that indicates that a process change in your urgent care department could improve margins and increase patient satisfaction (see case study).

Don't settle for just putting numbers on a piece of paper. You are reporting the value of your program, so the numbers mean more than just the numeric value. They represent value to the organization, satisfaction, ROI, and process improvement. The context of the numbers is critical. The number of current users of the system is meaningless, but the number of users as a percentage of all possible users is meaningful. The number of reports run each quarter just means you are good at input/output; you have no idea if anything valuable was actually created as a result of those reports.

But the impact those reports had on decisions or customers speak to the core of your business.

Case Study: The Power of Analytics

Dean Health System's journey to value through analytics started with a lean process improvement initiative. "Dean Health knew they had an opportunity to improve care and patient satisfaction," says Jennifer Close, VP of operations. Close led the analytics for Dean. Close had a long history of experience in payer analytics; she knew that analytics could offer a great deal of value, but was surprised at how little providers were using these tools. The lean process improvement that Dean Clinics started offered Close the opportunity to complete the analytics that she knew could provide great value to Dean as well as their patients.

As with many providers, Dean found themselves with tight margins and FTE strapped. They felt it necessary to improve the processes associated with urgent care (UC) utilization. Historically, their urgent care department was staffed heavily with providers. As they looked at the types of visits they had in UC, staffing physicians seemed overzealous compared to the acuity of the typical visit. Their analysis confirmed suspicions. They found that approximately 80 percent of their urgent care visits were of low acuity and didn't require the complex clinical decision making that required a physician.

Historically, patients had experienced access issues with getting an appointment the same day with their primary care provider (PCP). They had been "trained" to go to the urgent care and not even attempt to get an appointment. Using both medical record data and observational data from the nurses and physicians, analysis showed that in many cases the patients could have seen their provider the same day. In addition, they found that patients did not need to be seen by a physician at all; their concerns were appropriate to be addressed by a registered nurse or nurse practitioner.

As a result of this analysis, Dean introduced a nurse triage model much like their emergency department. This model ensured that the right provider was used for the acuity of the situation. If the patient presented with a complex history and symptomology, a physician was called in. If the patient presented with a symptoms of a urinary tract infection (UTI) or ear infection it was handled by a nurse practitioner.

The results were impressive, particularly with patient satisfaction. The patients were either given a same-day appointment with their primary care provider, or if an urgent care visit was needed, they received the right care at the right time, getting them in and out, and on with their day, quicker. "Analytics helped Dean see where they had opportunity," says Close. "Reports alone wouldn't have helped see this."

Urgent care triage wasn't the only place that Dean used analytics to improve. Just as impressive was the analytic approach to the management of their high blood pressure population. Dean participates with the Wisconsin Collaborative of Healthcare Quality (WCHQ). Part of that involved tracking BP control for their patients. Historically, Dean had had trouble managing it, even though they had been reporting to their physicians for three years. The analysis that Close's team completed found a high number of even-numbered readings (i.e., 150/70), but during a chart review, they discovered that the numbers were often being rounded up. They found that when the initial readings were high, a second reading often wasn't completed, or if it was completed, it wasn't always recorded, or was recorded in the notes section of the medical record. Process improvements were put in place after this initial analysis. They extended the vitals field for a second reading. A BP alert would prompt a nurse to take a second reading in five minutes if the first was over 140/90. Most impactful, they couldn't exit the medical record until they entered a second reading.

More analysis was completed on the process for seeing or managing patients with high blood pressure. Many times it was found that a protocol change was called for but wasn't documented. Dean's process improvements for BP control required that when a change in protocol was required, such as starting or changing medications, it was documented in the medical record where it could be captured. Small changes like this meant a big change to BP control for Dean. As Close said, "Reporting for BP management was ubiquitous. They had been doing it for three years with no change in procedures because it wasn't understood how they could change or what was needed for change."

Today, Dean Health continues its efforts using the power of analytics to impact its patients' lives and to deliver better care, faster. "Just reporting data won't get you there," says Close. "You have to use analytics to see beyond the sample size of one patient."

## CHAPTER 7

Gauging Your Readiness for BI

C hange is hard. Everywhere you look there are books, programs, and videos that are meant to help people change for the better. If it's so hard for an individual to change his or her behavior, an organizational change can feel impossible. Ask any business intelligence (BI) practitioner what the hardest part about implementing a BI program is and he or she will likely tell you it's the cultural shift that is required. You heard it from Darren Taylor in the case study in Chapter 4. In 2010 in an interview with *Computer World*, Gartner analyst Patrick Meehan said that BI programs should be "cultural transformations of the business, not IT projects."

Almost every client I have ever worked with or any peer that I have ever spoken to about BI has voiced similar opinions. For years, many of us went on working and implementing BI programs without a second thought to the organization's ability to embrace the change. It was a given that if you provided the organization with better information via an easy-to-use tool everyone would jump at the chance to learn it, right?

As it turns out, that's not so true. A case in point, a personal experience clearly demonstrates the need to understand the organization's preparedness. I was working diligently along with the rest of the BI and IT (information technology) team to implement a new BI tool. The excitement throughout the organization was tangible. The previous reporting tool was difficult to use and suffered from performance issues. The return on investment (ROI) for switching was even great. I felt really comfortable that the organization would continue to support the BI efforts after the implementation of the new tool. I couldn't have been more wrong.

Once the new tool was released, and people got used to it (that's a whole different story), the support for the larger BI effort dissipated quickly and significantly. The organization got what it wanted, and although the people liked the idea of "better reporting and analytics," they were not really prepared to support a multiyear effort to do that work. What I failed to recognize were the other factors at play in the organization. There were many other changes happening, taking valuable resources away from the BI effort. We were in the midst of a sudden downward shift financially, something the organization hadn't experienced in years. The most impactful, though, was a sudden change in executive leadership. I failed to assess the organization's readiness, willingness, and preparedness to take on another enterprise-level project along with everything else. I was resting on my laurels because of the successful deployment of the BI tool.

What I understand now is that preparing your organization for the change that BI brings is a big part of the job. To prepare you have to make sure that you know where the organization stands in its ability to adapt to change. As a result of this experience, I created this method of operationalizing the analysis of intervening variables to the success of the BI program. Since this experience, and because of this readiness model, I haven't been surprised by shifts in the organizational dynamic.

Even if you are perfectly prepared and you executed flawlessly on the tenets of healthcare BI, you still run a significant risk of being unsuccessful because of the organizational shift that is required. Thankfully, organizational research has been going on for decades. Although none of the research I have found is specific to BI implementations, the basic premise of organizational change applies to BI projects just as it would to other large enterprise projects. The groundbreaking research on organizational change was published in a 1994 issue of *Fortune* by Thomas A. Stewart. The article entitled "Rate your Readiness to Change" discusses the cultural implications of change for any organization. "People and culture—the human systems of a company—are what make or break any change initiative in a company" (Stewart, 1994). Stewart reports in the article that the most cited obstacles to change were employee resistance and dysfunctional corporate culture.

In his article, Stewart included a brief assessment to allow readers to rate their organization's readiness for change. Stewart indicates that the value associated with the assessment is twofold; it first demonstrates your business's viability with taking on the change, and second, gives you a list of things to focus on to improve the likelihood of taking on the change. The readiness to change scale is relatively simple. There are 17 key elements of change readiness:

1. Sponsorship
2. Leadership
3. Motivation
4. Direction
5. Measurements
6. Organizational content
7. Processes/function
8. Competitor benchmarking
9. Customer focus
10. Risk reward
11. Organizational structure
12. Communication
13. Organizational hierarchy
14. Prior experience with change
15. Morale

16. Innovation
17. Decision making

You rate your organization on high, medium, or low scale for each of these. The end rating gives you an indicator of how well your organization will adapt to a change of this scale (Stewart, 1994).

Tip: Take the Readiness-to-Change Assessment

Go to our companion website (www.wiley.com/go/healthcarebi) for more information and to take the assessment.

But that is only one part of the puzzle. The other part is how well prepared your organization is to take on a BI effort. We have walked through all of the tenets of healthcare BI. To assess your preparedness I have created a questionnaire that will rate you and your organization's ability to move ahead with BI (see Table 7.1).

If you indicate "yes" it means that you currently have this activity in your organization. "No" indicates that you do not do the activity in your organization. If you indicate "in progress" it means that the effort isn't complete but you have started. Check the most appropriate response for each question.

To complete the questionnaire, have the BI leader and the executive sponsor take the time to complete it together. There will likely be some conversation but they should agree on the final answer. For each "yes" you marked, give yourself two points, for each "no" you marked, give yourself zero points and for each "in progress" you marked, give yourself one point. Truthfulness is important for this assessment to work. Many of these questions are difficult to answer; questions about whether

TABLE 7.1 Healthcare BI Maturity

	Yes	No	In Progress

Data Quality

Do you have agreed-upon definitions for your data?

Do you manage metadata?

Do you have a data governance function operating?

Do users trust the data?

Leadership and Sponsorship

Do you have an assigned BI Leader?

Is the leader well respected throughout the
   organization?

Do you have more than one sponsor?

Do you have grassroots support?

Technology and Architecture

Do you currently follow ETL best practices?

Do you have a data model?

Is your hardware right-sized for performance and
   scalability?

Do you have a trusted IT leader?

Value

Does the organization perceive BI as a value today?

Do you have good user adoption?

Do users feel that BI is critical to their ability to do
   their job?

Does your BI function report up through the
   business?

Assessing Readiness

Has your organization made successful
   enterprise-wide changes in the past?

Does your organization believe data can help make
   better decisions?

Is your organization committed to data
   management?

Is your organization prepared to make the changes
   necessary to adopt BI?

TABLE 7.2 Maturity Stages

Your Score	Your Stage
0–10	Stage 1
11–30	Stage 2
31–40	Stage 3

or not a leader is well respected, or even whether the hardware is right-sized, can open old wounds. It's essential that everyone understands that doing this assessment isn't about placing blame but about moving forward to deliver a great product to end-users.

When you combine the tenets assessment with the readiness-to-change assessment, you end up with a diagnostic tool to understand where you are today (see Table 7.2). The power of that tool is to compare where you are now with where you want to be in the future, and then create a step-wise approach to get there.

Each data point gives us insight, and when combined helps us understand how to best proceed. Each box on the scorecard requires a slightly different approach (see Figure 7.1).

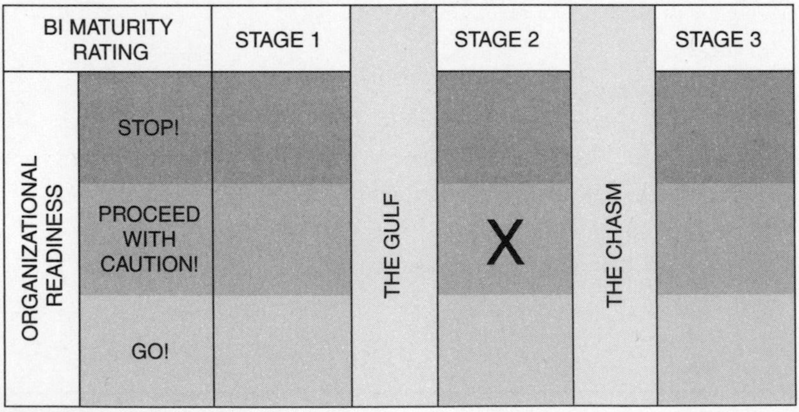

BI MATURITY RATING		STAGE 1	THE GULF	STAGE 2	THE CHASM	STAGE 3
ORGANIZATIONAL READINESS	STOP!					
	PROCEED WITH CAUTION!			X		
	GO!					

FIGURE 7.1 Healthcare BI Readiness Scorecard

Depending on where you score, the resolution needed to move you forward will vary greatly. It's not as simple as saying that if you score very low on the readiness-to-change scale that you should stop what you're doing, even though the result implies that.

Stop

Some simple guidelines to follow for each level of readiness for change; if you are in the Stop stage you will want to address the areas you scored lowest on to increase the change readiness in your organization. During this time you may also want to complete some small pilot projects that deliver good business value.

Stage 1

This is perhaps the easiest of stages to address. Most likely you just have an idea about what you want to do but have made no actual progress. After taking the readiness-to-change assessment, you recognize that your company is not ready for a BI project. Your next step is education. If there is a shared understanding of BI then perhaps your company will be more prepared to invest in a project. Start with a grassroots effort to raise awareness. These conversations are best between you and your peers. This will gain momentum for the project at the layer that does the majority of the work. You may also want to attempt to get some executive or influencer into your inner circle. It's also a good idea to determine how many rogue spreadsheets your organization has. Many people in the BI industry refer to these rogue spreadsheets as *spreadmarts*. The idea is that someone created a spreadsheet and then it eventually became the source of the data. Determining the frequency of this risky practice will help you determine how much work there is to get it under control. Rogue spreadsheets cost your organization

181

real money. That lack of consistency or application of business rules for these spreadsheets can lead to poor decisions based on flawed data. According to TDWI (the Data Warehousing Institute), the median cost of spreadmarts to each organization is $780,000 annually (1105 Media, 2010).

Once you have made some inroads with your educational efforts and assessed your rogue spreadsheets, take the assessments again. If the score has changed, then you are ready to move forward. If not, keep addressing the areas you scored low on until you can move to the next level.

Steps for getting out of Stage 1: Stop

1. Start a grassroots effort of educating peers about how BI could help make their jobs easier.
2. Gain executive support—the more the better.
3. Estimate how many rogue spreadsheets are running your business.
4. Retake the assessments to determine the level of progress.

Tip: The Gulf

The Data Warehousing Institute (TDWI) came out with a BI maturity model a number of years ago. In their assessment, they point out two large obstacles that impede an organization's ability to move forward with BI, the first being the gulf. "To cross the Gulf, organizations must convert users from spreadmarts to more standardized views of information" (1105 Media, 2010). What that means is that we must find a way to manage our data for consistency's sake. If you run into the gulf, it will probably occur between the Stages 1 and 2 of the healthcare BI maturity.

Stage 2

Because you have created some of your BI program, now is the time to attempt to regain support that you had when you started. To do this, first you must do a current-state assessment. These efforts are the "state of the union" for your BI program. You should start by documenting usage statistics: specifically look to determine what reports are used by whom and how often. If there are reports that are not used frequently, determine if they are still needed or could be combined with others. Next, identify the number of spreadmarts currently in use. Spreadmarts can be destructive to the primary goals of BI, so you will need to balance the need for the data to be readily available while still using consistent definitions. Spreadmarts are usually created because it was quicker and easier than going the traditional route within the organization. That means that you have an opportunity and an obligation to ensure that your processes are as streamlined as possible.

Finally, reengage your executive sponsor or find a new one. The best way to get some sponsorship back is to choose a small project that will deliver some business value (which will likely help with funding and executive perceptions). Don't bite off more than you can chew; the idea here is to show that you can make progress. Select something that doesn't require much input from disparate departments. Because you are in Stage 1 in your organizational readiness to change, you are not in a position to be able to ask others for assistance. The best-case scenario is they will say no, and the worst case is they will sabotage your efforts. It's best to stick with a well-documented data domain that a good analyst could tap into for some discernible business value. A great example is using clinical data, and an analyst who understands it. Clinical data is a great option because many organizations have had limited access to it. An even more powerful scenario would be combining clinical and financial data together. An analysis that many healthcare organizations would like to do but can't because of data issues is to assess the cost of procedures against the clinical effectiveness of the procedure. If you can do an analysis of this type, then you can take the assessments again to gauge your progress.

Steps for getting out of Stage 2: Stop
1. Complete a current state assessment.
2. Ensure good sponsorship.
3. Do a pilot project with high business value.

Tip: Beware the Chasm

At this point you will need to be wary of the chasm. Some of the key attributes of the chasm are:

- Business volatility: Rapid changes, whether they are strategic or leadership
- Reconciling metrics: Constantly comparing and validating metrics
- Transition to corporate IT: Shift from distributed to centralized IT
- Making BI pervasive: Goal to increase the knowledge of the organization through BI
- Report chaos: Many reports with competing data from multiple systems
- Architectural inflexibility: Current technology platform will not support BI initiatives

Unlike the gulf, these challenges are much more difficult to address. Many BI projects fall into the chasm never to be seen again. It's not unusual to see the budget investments dwindle with the level of interest. Your user base starts to decrease, and at this point new rogue spreadsheets start popping up in a department or two. To avoid this fate you must ensure that you have strong leadership and sponsorship from the business side; ideally your BI department resides in the business. The only way to crawl back out of chasm is to show the business the true value of an enterprise view of consolidated data, and that answer can't be about the number of users or number of reports run. That answer has to be about what decisions are made, who is impacted, what changes can be made, and how you can compete better (1105 Media, 2010). If you experience the chasm it will likely be between Stages 2 and 3. Keep in mind that you can be in the chasm for a long period of time and it takes a concerted effort to make your way out.

Stage 3

You have created a lot of work, but somewhere along the way support for the project decreased. This can happen because of the chasm or as a result of the implications of your organization's readiness to change. If it is the chasm, then you will want to determine what part of the chasm is affecting you the most. Is it business volatility, reconciling metrics, transition to corporate IT, making BI pervasive, report chaos, or architectural inflexibility? If it doesn't seem to be the chasm, then it's likely to be one of the key elements of the readiness-to-change assessment. This can be a tricky hill to climb. Review the scores on the readiness-to-change assessment and have them validated by someone else. Sometimes another person's perspective is all that is needed.

You will want to tread lightly for your next step. Step back and make sure that you are reasonably sure about the cause of your situation (chasm or the organization's readiness to change).

It's never a bad idea to attempt to regain support by showing value, as you will see that I recommend that often. The advantage you have as a Stage 3 is your ability to show value because so much of it already exists. Perhaps now is the time to create your portal strategy, or redesign some static reports to a more visually impactful presentation. It may also be a good time to spend some time educating both your peer group and the executives on any areas that were lower in the healthcare BI maturity assessment. It's not enough to rest on your laurels; keep plugging away until you get to a go stage.

Steps to getting out of Stage 3: Stop

1. Are you in the chasm? Review the factors that indicate the chasm and decide.
2. If you are not in the chasm go back to the readiness to change assessment and review your low scores. Focus your efforts there.
3. Deliver value and continue to educate the organization on the value of BI.

Proceed with Caution

The small pilot projects you attempted in the stop phase will help to make your case to move to the next phase—"yellow" or proceed with caution. In the yellow phase you should focus solely on the areas that you scored low on. This will help address the areas of weakness for your organization. Change is possible at this phase, but it's difficult.

Stage 1

You have a blank slate on which to work and some support to move forward. Because support is tepid, you will need to plan appropriately the work to show executives the potential value.

Now is the time to do a strategic assessment and complete a road map. This should take between 12 and 14 weeks. Your first order of business is to ensure that this is a good strategic step for your organization. To do this you must determine the cost of keeping things at the status quo. In other words, how much does it cost the organization in actual dollars to have high-level analysts running reports? How much does it cost to have a series of spreadmarts in use? How much does it cost to not have a data quality program in place with a shared corporate lexicon? This type of planning can be achieved through a road map exercise, which I address in detail in Chapter 4.

Steps to getting out of Stage 1: Proceed with caution
1. Do a road map to plan the effort for the next 18 to 24 months.
2. Do an ROI analysis.
3. Don't forget to show value often.

Tip: Map Your Destiny

Check out Chapter 4 and our companion website (www.wiley.com/go/healthcarebi) for more information about road mapping and a downloadable template to get you started.

Stage 2

You are halfway there. Most companies fall in Stage 2 of the maturity model, so you are in good company. The good news for you is that you have made progress on your BI maturity and have some support from your organization. Now you will want to focus on your weak areas so you can get to the next stage.

Review your scores and determine which of the five tenets you scored the lowest on. Then come up with a plan of action to address those weaknesses. To continue the support you have from your executives, you may want to adopt the maturity model as your reference point to executives to demonstrate progress. Simply take the assessment every six months to a year to determine if the changes you have made result in progress along the maturity model.

Again, you are at risk to fall into the chasm, so I would recommend being conservative in your push to move through the maturity model, especially if you are scoring low on the healthcare BI assessment (scores in the low 20s). Exercise some caution and stay the course for a while until you have mastered this level. The chasm can be difficult to escape from, and you don't want to be put into that trap.

Steps to getting out of Stage 2: Proceed with caution

1. Focus on low scores in the healthcare BI maturity assessment and try to increase them.
2. Create a plan of action to address the weak points and reassess every six months.
3. Stay conservative. Show some value that doesn't put the BI program at risk.

Case Study: Stage 2: Regression toward the Mean

In my consulting work I usually start a new client with an assessment. This helps me get a lot of information in a short amount of time. What this has taught me is that many clients overestimate their abilities and underestimate the organizational impact. They will score themselves higher on things than I would score them on, and in some respects end up at a higher overall score as a result.

The value of these assessments is to gauge your status and your organization's readiness to adapt, but if the scores aren't reflective of the reality then it's a fool's game. I remember a number of years ago I started working with a new health plan. The clients had recently made a BI tool purchase and were looking to get started with a more complete BI program. My method for guiding assessments is to get the group of people that will be the most influential in the BI program in a room to come to a consensus on their responses to each question. This allows for group "buy-in" of the final scores, but also shows everyone in the room where the differences are. If your IT team members are telling me that they are very advanced in managing metadata but your users are telling me they have never seen it, that's a gap that needs to be addressed.

In this particular instance the room was full with analysts, end-users, IT staff, and the executive sponsor. In answering almost every question, the individuals disagreed with one another. They were far apart in their views on where they were in BI maturity and on the organization's readiness to change. Red flags were going up for me all over the place. My fight-or-flight response was screaming *run*. In the end, they rated themselves as a Stage 2 (although they probably should have been in the high Stage 1 under "proceed with caution").

After the meeting, the project manager approached me and said, "That was a very interesting meeting. That's the first time we have ever talked about any of those things. I think a lot of people were rating us higher than they should have been because the executive sponsor was in the room."

Indeed he was right. The organization struggled to do the basics, and in the end is still struggling with trying to create and release an enterprise data warehouse.

About six months later I was working with another organization that was keen to get started. The problem was the enthusiasm for the project was limited to the project manager and a vice president, who didn't feel he could play the role of executive sponsor. Their score was Stage 1, and their readiness to change was firmly in the stop stage. In this instance their truthfulness was represented in the scores but they were unable to equate that to change. They never got the project off the ground.

The point in both of these stories is that one or the other isn't sufficient. Both pieces, your maturity in the healthcare BI tenets and the organization's ability to adapt to change, will impact your ability to be successful with any BI initiative.

Figure 7.2 will help you communicate the value of these assessments. As you make progress on both fronts (readiness to change and healthcare BI maturity) you can retake the assessments and track your progress. Demonstrating that progress via this graph will show users and executives the fruits of the labor.

Stage 3

For those of you in Stage 3, the "proceed with caution" stage can be a bit frustrating. You have likely enjoyed a position of autonomy in the past and succeeded in developing an enterprise data warehouse with strategic use of your organization's

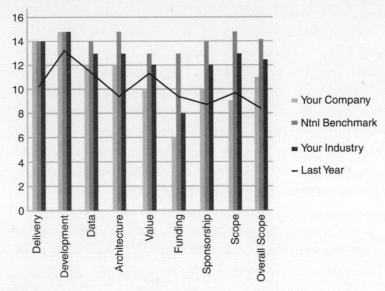

FIGURE 7.2 Maturity over Time

information resources. Perhaps recently you have started to experience a "chilly" reception with your executive sponsor. It may not be a reflection of you or the program; it may be a reflection of the increased pressure that all healthcare organizations feel when considering an investment. It's best to stay the course here. Continue to deliver good business value and plan your work accordingly. Review your scores on both assessments to determine what is most impeding your ability to move forward. Make modest attempts to address any outstanding issues. You are so far along on the maturity model, so there isn't a big push to improve the scores (although work in that direction will always be worthwhile).

The Go Stage

Congratulations! Regardless of where you fall in the healthcare BI maturity model you have the full support of your organization behind you. In the Go phase you are positioned to succeed with a BI project. You should still spend some time focusing on any of the lagging indicators of readiness to change, but your primary focus should be moving yourself toward Healthcare BI maturity. This is a big win and really sets you up for success, as long as you take precise actions along the maturity model phases. There are fewer negative implications of the organization's readiness to change, so we will not review each phase in detail. Your focus should be how you move your organization along the maturity model. Key considerations you should make:

- Always plan your work. Complete a strategic assessment and create a road map that covers a minimum of 18 months of releases.
- Watch for symptoms of the gulf or the chasm.
- Consistently review your scores on both assessments and retake them when you hit milestones.
- Deliver value quickly and frequently to maintain executive support.
- Show business value if you are not sure of your next step. Unleash a talented analyst on a rich, untapped data domain, and just stand back.

It may seem obvious that your organization's state of readiness is a factor in the successful delivery of a BI program; truthfully it is but one facet of a diamond. To complete the analogy, a well-designed and implemented BI program is like a well-cut diamond, very valuable. A poorly designed BI program is like a poorly cut diamond, not much more than an expensive trinket. Although it seems relatively easy to place your organization on this continuum, it is not the solution by itself. It is simply another piece of information to help you down your road to BI success.

In Chapter 9 we discuss in much more detail how to move forward once you are at the Go stage.

Notes

Stewart, T.A. (1994). Rate Your Organizations Readiness to Change. *Fortune*, February 7, 1994.

1105 Media. (2010, August 15). TDWI. Retrieved December 2, 2011, from The Data Warehousing Institute, A Division of 1105 Media: http://tdwi .org/pages/best-practices-awards/tdwi-best-practice-awards-2010-winners .aspx.

CHAPTER 8

Future Trends in Healthcare BI

The best thing about the future is that it comes one day at a time.

—Abraham Lincoln

Odds are, the reason you are reading this book is because of the Health Information Technology for Economic Clinical Health (HITECH) Act of 2009. Before that point, business intelligence (BI) in healthcare was something only the big guys did. Few people could have seen that data would play such a pivotal role before 2008. The key difference is the increase in adoption of electronic health records (EHR). Although we had been talking about adopting EHR for decades, broader adoption eluded us. The HITECH Act of 2009 presented financial incentives too good for many organizations to pass up, which is how we got here. It's not glamorous and, for many of us, it happened begrudgingly, but the HITECH Act has forced a national conversation about the role of data in healthcare. This conversation is driving changes in how healthcare organizations manage data, what they measure from it, and how they track outcomes over time.

It is hard to predict the future in an industry that has seen such rapid change in such a short time. I don't see the pace of change slowing very soon, though. The nature of the requirements associated with Meaningful Use and Accountable Care

Organization require a continued and increasing investment in data. But beyond the things that the government requires us to do, there are other variables that impact the future of healthcare BI. This multifaceted industry will see pressure come from other activities such as healthcare information exchanges, rapid innovations in technology (influx of mobile devices for example), and, perhaps most impactful, the population that we deliver care to.

Four key trends will impact the future of healthcare BI; in reality, some of them are impacting us today.

1. Integration of data from disparate sources (i.e., healthcare information exchanges).
2. The changing population of healthcare consumers is ushering in a whirlwind of change. This new population demands more information and is willing to seek it through social media and the interactive web (i.e., Web 2.0). This requires us to modify data privacy and security policies.
3. Mobile technologies for business intelligence.
4. "Big data" and analytics will drive home the value equation for healthcare BI.

EHRs change the data game for healthcare BI; EHR brings us one step closer to the holistic view of a patient or member. The remaining challenge is the ability to integrate the disparate sources of data in healthcare, as seen in Figure 8.1. Without that integration, we will always have a siloed view of a patient. Without that integration, the value of BI to a healthcare organization will always be limited. The only way we can get out of this siloed view of data is to change our shared view of who owns data and why. We can no longer control the data that our organizations possess and feel good about the care we are providing to our members and patients. Each one of these silos

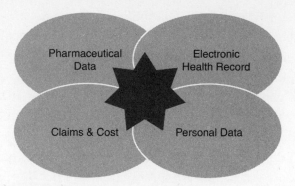

FIGURE 8.1 Disparate Healthcare Data Sources

is just one view of the data; separately they have limited value, but together they can change healthcare.

Web 2.0 and Social Media

The next generation of patients that is becoming part of the traditional insurance pool views and consumes information in a very different way. This is the generation that readily advertises its relationship status and clinical information to "friends" and "followers" instead of (or before) telling a healthcare practitioner. These patients seek their information through the Internet. Their technical prowess is part of their birthright. They have different perspectives on security and privacy. The push isn't just in how we deliver healthcare differently, which is important, but how we deliver information about health.

This isn't traditional BI, but Web 2.0 and social media are offering a type of information that wasn't always available before. But how does this impact the future of BI? If patients are entering health information onto websites such as Facebook, things like drug reactions (e.g., nausea after chemo), or any other symptom—isn't that something that would be good to have in an EHR?

As I consider all of the information, the shifts, and changes both in healthcare delivery as well as socially and culturally, I see that the future of healthcare BI is with the patient. Today much of the focus is on the healthcare organizations, such as hospitals and health plans, and employer groups such as the member's employer, but there is no doubt that as the technically savvy generation comes of age and consumes more healthcare, they will demand a more robust, transparent, and contextually driven source of healthcare information.

Four years ago my sister, on her 41st birthday, learned she had breast cancer. The diagnosis was shocking and happened so quickly that my sister felt ill equipped and underinformed; she immediately went to Google. The information there was terrifying. It spelled out every horrible thing that could possibly happen, regardless of the odds. Without context, specifically her type of cancer and the stage she was in, the information was just distracting and distressing. Thankfully, she understood quickly that the level of information was not helpful, and she stopped herself from doing random Internet searches. But she did use the Internet for other purposes. She reached out to her broader network. All of that support and encouragement came from geographically dispersed friends and family as she shared her experiences on Facebook. She was able to inform her friends of her progress, include pictures of successes, and feel the encouragement from people on her toughest days. The support and encouragement of friends and family is something that most researchers will agree is helpful in the healing process.

My sister had a frightening and one-sided experience with Google, which is the risk you run with search engines that don't allow for the interaction like Web 2.0 does, where you are encouraged to interact with either a group of similar people or create better context for searching (such as symptom checkers on sites like WebMD). I had a different Google experience at a

Signs and Symptoms of a Cervical Radiculopathy C5-C8

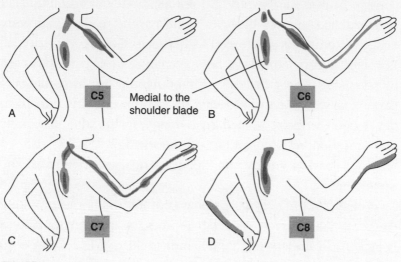

FIGURE 8.2 Googling

doctor's office. Perhaps as a result of spending too many hours slumped over my beautiful but poorly designed desk feverishly typing out this book, I herniated my C5 disc. For any of you who have had this injury, it's incredibly painful. It made it nearly impossible to type, or hold my own head up, and the drugs that were prescribed brought any critical thinking skills to a complete stop. So I sought out a specialist, hoping for some miraculous cure that would ensure I would meet all my deadlines. What I got was Google. Don't misunderstand me, I spoke with the physician. He was clear about the diagnosis and the prognosis, as well as the treatment. But when he sat down to explain to me what happened, he turned the computer screen in my direction and went to Google and typed in "cervical radiculopathy" (medical term for the nerve pain I was experiencing as a result of the herniation). I asked him "Did you just Google?" His response, in a tone that implied the obvious, "Yes, I did." What appeared before me is shown in Figure 8.2.

Google per se isn't the future, but mass access to useful, correct, and available health information is. Web 2.0 is also part of that equation. Google is still part of the original web, and it remains very one-sided for patients seeking information. But, in this instance, where my clinician served as the business rules engine, it provided me with the right information that was contextually important and easy to understand. I would have never been so bold as to diagnose myself, but after diagnosis and prescriptions I have all of the information I will ever need on the injury, treatment, and connections to others with the same ailment.

Today, for the average patient, little information is provided to them. You receive your lab reports, in a language only a clinician can understand. As an individual you have a right to create a personal health record (PHR) and incorporate that into your EHR from your clinic or hospital, but generally only those who deal with chronic diseases go to that extent because you become responsible for the management of it.

Without the focus on easy-to-understand information, patients have to do more legwork or reach for less-than-valid sources. We have to find a way, today in BI, to make the information we provide to patients accessible. Because if we don't someone will. Here's a perfect case in point. I had my annual physical this summer. The physician took a lot of blood to run a number of tests. Figure 8.3 shows what the lab report looked like.

Along with this cryptic lab report I got a two-sentence letter back from my physician that said: "The results of your recent lab blood work were NORMAL. A copy of your results is enclosed for your convenience." I looked at that report a number of times over the next few weeks. Something was bothering me; it wasn't the actual results (because for the most part I didn't understand them), but then I realized that's what was bothering me—the lack of understanding. This felt like an attempt to be

Component	Latest Ref Rng	9/14/2011
Sodium	133–144 mmol/L	142
Potassium	3.4–5.3 mmol/L	4.0
Chloride	94–109 mmol/L	106
Carbon Dioxide	20–32 mmol/L	24
Anion Gap	6–17 mmol/L	12
Glucose	60–99 mg/dL	90
Urea Nitrogen	5–24 mg/dL	12
Creatinine	0.52–1.04 mg/dL	0.70
GFR Estimate	Low: > 60 mL/min/1.7m2	> 90
GFR Estimate If Black	Low: > 60 mL/min/1.7m2	> 90
Calcium	8.5–10.4 mg/dL	9.3
Bilirubin Total	0.2–1.3 mg/dL	0.3
Albumin	3.9–5.1 g/dL	4.7
Protein Total	6.8–8.8 g/dL	7.5
Alkaline Phosphatase	40–150 U/L	53
ALT	0–50 U/L	14
AST	0–45 U/L	19
WBC	4.0–11.0 10e9/L	7.0
RBC Count	3.8–5.2 10e12/L	4.24
Hemoglobin	11.7–15.7 g/dL	12.9
Hematocrit	35.0–47.0 %	37.5
MCV	78–100 fl	88
MCH	26.5–33.0 pg	30.4
MCHC	31.5–36.5 g/dL	34.4
RDW	10.0 15.0 %	12.2
Platelet Count	150–450 10e9/L	265
Specimen Description		Serum
Lyme Screen IgG and IgM		Test value: < 0.75.... Interpretation: Negative.... If you highly suspect Lyme...
Tissue Transglutaminase Antibody IgA	0–3.9 U/mL	< 1.0...
Tissue Transglutaminase Aby IgG	0–5.9 U/mL	1.0
TSH	0.4–5.0 mU/L	2.43
T4 Free	0.70–1.85 ng/dL	0.96
FSH	IU/L	3.5
Lutropin	IU/L	4.9
Rheumatoid Factor	0–14 IU/mL	8

FIGURE 8.3 Laura's Lab Report

transparent and provide information, but it's not information if the recipient can't consume it. That is why the specialist used Google—because he understood that for me to consume this information I needed it presented to me in a way that I could understand.

With the innovation of BI tools there is no reason why the lab reports we send to patients should ever look like this. I find it frustrating, because I know what's possible. But when I look at my lab report I don't always see normal. A number of these results are very near the top of the reference range. Wouldn't it make sense to track these over time? I am not sure, because I am not a clinician, but as a BI professional I wish these lab reports looked like Figure 8.4.

While BI professionals everywhere were busy with our heads down, something started to happen. The influx of social media and the change in values associated with sharing personal health information has changed the dynamic of information security. Today, websites such as PatientsLikeMe.com allow patients with chronic conditions to share what medicines they take, interactions, effectiveness, and all other types of information with patients with the same condition. The potential is amazing for patients who are afflicted with the same condition, but Patientslikeme.com has a different perspective on how healthcare privacy has impacted research and care. The site's "openness philosophy" is the building block of its mission, and does usher in a new way to think about healthcare information. The mission of its openness philosophy is "speeding up the pace of research and fixing a broken healthcare system" (Patientslikeme.com, 2012). Its openness philosophy goes on to discuss the impact of this "broken healthcare system":

Currently, most healthcare data is inaccessible due to privacy regulations or proprietary tactics. As a result, research is slowed, and the development of breakthrough treatments

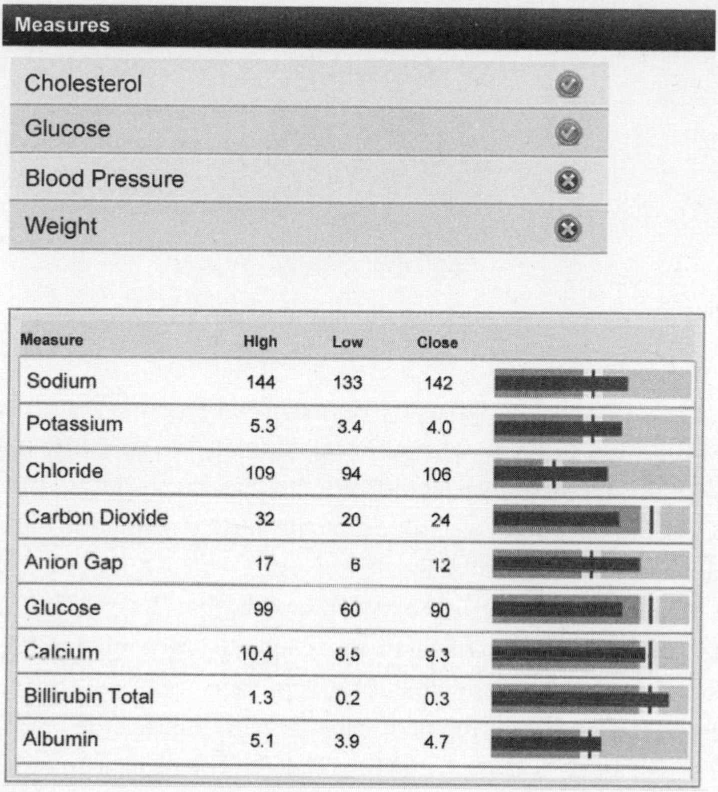

Measures	
Cholesterol	✔
Glucose	✔
Blood Pressure	✖
Weight	✖

Measure	High	Low	Close	
Sodium	144	133	142	
Potassium	5.3	3.4	4.0	
Chloride	109	94	106	
Carbon Dioxide	32	20	24	
Anion Gap	17	6	12	
Glucose	99	60	90	
Calcium	10.4	8.5	9.3	
Billirubin Total	1.3	0.2	0.3	
Albumin	5.1	3.9	4.7	

FIGURE 8.4 Laura's New Lab Report

*takes decades. Patients also can't get the information they
need to make important treatment decisions. But it doesn't
have to be that way. When you and thousands like you share
your data, you open up the healthcare system. You learn
what's working for others. You improve your dialogue with
your doctors. Best of all, you help bring better treatments to
market in record time.*

(Patientslikeme.com, 2012)

This type of information and support in a website, outside
of a brick-and-mortar entity (although PatientsLikeMe.com has
a strong clinical focus), changes the dynamic between patients

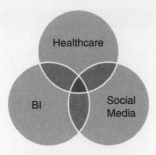

FIGURE 8.5 Healthcare, Business Intelligence, and Social Media

and their physician. What that means for BI is that we need to start thinking in terms of making data available to patients in a way that is easy to understand. We will have to redefine privacy and security to take advantage of the influx of health data for better outcomes (see Figure 8.5).

Where does that leave the hospital that has traditionally been responsible for most of the clinically focused healthcare information? The role will still be a primary one, as physicians will always be at the heart of care delivery, and their organizations will have to be at the heart of data acquisition, storage, and management. But what will be increasingly important is the ability to present the information to a broader audience in a way that is easy to understand. In addition, we will have many new security and privacy questions. Today, we hold these data with the highest regard, as we should, but we will be pressed to continue to preserve while also share. It is a consideration that many of us haven't been presented with yet.

Mobile Technologies for Healthcare BI

The adoption curve for new gadgets has changed drastically in the past decade. The pace of change is mind-boggling, and we just continue to adopt all the latest and greatest. It hasn't always been that way. I was a teenager when we first got a microwave. The gadget looked positively space-age in our farm-house kitchen. I was an early adopter, even going to the library to get a recipe book for microwaves. I tried cooking everything in that thing. My dad, for his part, just exclaimed every time it beeped, "These damn gadgets are always making noise." My father still feels the same about gadgets and complains incessantly about the influx of cell phones during holiday visits.

Gadgets are here to stay. You cannot argue that they have changed the way we live and work. Beyond cursing the things, we rely on them a great deal. We rely on them to help us remember, navigate our journey to a new destination, keep us in contact with work and loved ones, distract us while waiting, keep our calendars straight, and a litany of other activities.

But not all gadgets apply to all ways of life. When BI started going "mobile" lots of people asked me what value there would be in getting monthly reports on a teeny-tiny screen. Virtually none was always my answer, but it wasn't the right question. The right question is what value does having the information at your fingertips provide you? Stale information, something produced batch-style each month, is useless on your mobile device. That is the old way of looking at BI; that way is becoming more and more outdated every day.

I think back to my college days and my behavioral psychology class. The professor had a keen interest in biofeedback. He took the class down to a lab and hooked up some willing volunteers. The demonstration was easy; show the volunteers something that would increase their heart rate, and then have them practice watching the heart rate monitor to bring it back down regardless of stimuli. The idea is simple, the closer you get to an observed behavior (although in biofeedback it is an autonomic response) the better chance you have of addressing it. It's why we drag our puppies to their messes and why pills that make you sick after certain behavior (smoking or drinking) are popular.

Radio frequency identification (RFID) tags and mobile devices allow you to get as close to the observed behavior as possible. This technology provides hospitals the ability to track staff for easier paging, track clean linens, and even allow for tracking surgical devices during procedures.

Technology has no inherent value, except when it can completely change the way we work.

Analytics: More Than a Buzzword

I am educated as an applied analyst. All that really means is that I was trained how to analyze data that already existed somewhere. There are statistical models that control things such as intervening variable and selection bias. Much of my master's-level education focused on how bad data is and how I can still glean insights from it despite its errant nature. I remember the thrill I used to get when I found something that no one else saw. I thought that applied analytics was the way to the brave new world—that if everyone could do what I could, the world would be a better place.

I started in the corporate world before "analytics" was the next big thing. As a matter of fact, when I started, having the title of "analyst" meant something, rather than today's proliferation of the title to anyone who uses data. Much of my work in those early years had little to do with analytics and a lot to do with basic math. I was surprised at how few of the people I worked for couldn't apply a basic statistical model to data. My first year out of college I worked for a small hospital; my title was "research coordinator" but I was responsible for anything that had to do with data or analytics. I was even called on to create the calculation they used to assess pay raises. I remember spending time with the human resource director explaining the calculation and thinking, "Wow, I will never be out of a job as long as I have this skill set."

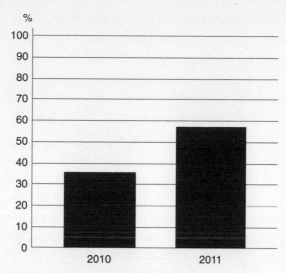

FIGURE 8.6 Increasing Demand for Analytics

Fast-forward more than a decade later and it's true; my skill set is in high demand. Today, to differentiate from the ubiquitous title of "analyst" many organizations are in search of the data "scientist" (see Figure 8.6.) The function is the same, with perhaps a bit more emphasis today on "big data," the idea that the data exists in such huge volumes that you have to understand how to navigate and analyze petabytes and beyond.

Be that as it may, we still have a large gap in most of our organizations (David Kiron, 2011). We still need to have the average manager be savvy enough to consume the analytics that the "data scientists" create. The gap is significant, and it puts most of our organizations at risk because we are not in a position to take full advantage of everything that our data can provide for us. Whether you call the person a data scientist or an analyst, if the average person can't take that information and do something with it, make a decision, or modify a process, then the role of analyst and the voluminous data is just an exercise in distraction.

In my experience the average organization has about 2 percent of its workforce who are true analysts (remember the user continuum). This 2 percent is usually in high demand. The challenge we have is how do we create an analytically driven organization? Most of our employees should have the ability to consume data in a way that they can use it, without everyone having to be trained as an analyst.

One of the definitions of BI, if you were to do an Internet search for it, is "The right information to the right person in the right way at the right time." I believe this applies just as much to the ability for organizations to broadly consume information as it does to BI. To be clear, BI and analytics are not the same thing. BI does not inherently provide smart data. BI is a process, a method, or a set of best practices for extracting, storing, transforming, and preparing data for usage by a broad audience. Analytics takes it a step further, using the data that is prepared by the BI function to find real value to the organization. BI enables analytics.

Creating a Data-Driven Organization

So with BI enabling an analytic function, how do we improve our organization's ability to consume information? With increased demand for experts in analytics but not enough of them to go around, what in the world can anyone do? In the short-term, organizations can:

- Force decisions to be quantified.
- Broaden your workforce data IQ.
- Demonstrate data through visualizations.
- Provide additional education.
- Hire analytical people.

The work begins at the top of the organization. Today, many of our organizations, both healthcare- and not healthcare-related, are driven by gut instincts. An enormous amount of research exists that examines the effectiveness of this method, much of it concluding that it isn't good. For healthcare organizations to really start to adopt the benefits of BI, they have to become a data-driven organization and that means the leaders of the organizations (perhaps you reading this book) must demand that any decision that impacts the organization be quantified. That isn't easy to do, particularly if you don't have the data, or access to the data, that is required. But if you think that it is the right way to go, then support a BI program in your organization so you can make data-driven decisions.

Staff Turnover Is a Likely Result of Becoming an Analytically Driven Organization

The next step is critically important and just as difficult. You have to increase your workforce's ability to understand data. This will likely come at a price, in staff turnover, as it did for a bank that adapted a sophisticated segmentation analysis. "The bank had moved from intuitive to fact-based decision making using analytics. It was interesting to learn from the CEO that this new way of running the bank was accompanied by a large turnover in personnel" (Watson, 2006).

Although Watson's quote is specific to the banking industry, it applies to any industry that attempts to shift from decisions by instinct to decisions from data. Changes in staffing aren't always a bad thing, as long as they happen for the right reasons. A strategic shift in how the organization consumes data is a good reason, in my opinion. But what if you could anticipate this impact and reduce its effect? You can. Help your employees by improving their ability to consume information in the way it will be provided to them. Help managers be ready to make data-driven decisions.

In one of my jobs I was asked to help people understand the value of data. The team I worked on was responsible for disseminating a government-mandated report to a large group of health plans. These reports were basic frequency statistics, a reference to sampling and demographic information. Many of the people who received this report weren't really sure what these numbers meant or how it impacted them. The team created a short class that we delivered via a web-meeting called "Business Stats 101." The courses took less than an hour and explained all of the statistics on the report and how to interpret them. The course was so popular that before long we were delivering it to other teams throughout the organization. What we found was that people were willing and interested to learn, when given the opportunity. You can duplicate that experience in your organization by creating a similar course that will better prepare your organization for consuming analytics.

Another important step is to ensure that you prepare information in a way that is highly consumable. A better-informed workforce is important, but there is no way you will reach everyone. If you commit to visualizing your data in a way that the average person can consume, you will improve your entire organization's ability to make data-driven decisions, and perhaps more importantly, provide them with the right tools to ask more informed questions. You can start by ensuring that your data has context, such as a benchmark or goal. When you look at a report you should be able to answer the question "So what?"

Data visualization is not just a fancy term for nice looking dashboards. It is an industry all in itself; perhaps most notably started by Edward Tufte. Tufte's story is one of passion. He is a Stanford-trained statistician, but felt so compelled by the importance of "information design" that he self-published his first book *Visual Display* by putting a second mortgage on his house. Tufte's books and courses are now wildly popular, and he is a big critic of much of the way organizations have evolved to share information.

> *The purpose of analytical displays of evidence is to assist thinking.*
>
> —Edward R. Tufte (Thralls, 2004)

Along with providing rich information through graphics and educating your workforce about data, analytics, and information, you will want to consider hiring more analytically minded people. Certainly in specific roles the analytic perspective is critical, but expanding that skill set from preferred to required for key roles will send a message that your organization is serious about becoming a data-driven organization.

Big Data and Why It Matters

Just like any other industry, BI has its trends. My approach is to wait it out, usually giving it a full year before I dedicate any significant consideration to the next "big" thing. In this case that's "Big" data. Big data started out as a trend, something you heard discussions about on Twitter or at cocktail parties full of data warehouse consultants. Big data is an evolution, as the definition will have to change over time as data continues to grow. It seems almost incomprehensible that data could get bigger, but it's bound to happen as we adopt EHR.

My challenge with big data is what big data means to healthcare is different from what it means to most other industries. Currently we are storing a lot less data than any other industry. We have an incredible amount of data wrapped up in our transactional systems such as the EHR. Some limitations exist for healthcare and how "big" big data will get because so much of the data that has value for us is qualitative data (e.g., nurse notes). Today, big data is defined as massive amounts, in the petabytes. Not that long ago, massive meant somewhere in the terabyte range. Definitions for big data will morph over time, and I believe that at some point in the future we will stop calling it *big* because it's just the amount of data we have. But just because we have more doesn't mean it's always better. There are implications to more data. It will force us to review data policies and reconsider the technology and methods that we use for data, and it will likely have organizational impacts as we attempt to extract value and disseminate that across the organization. I still highly encourage any organization that is looking down the barrel of big data to make sure that there is commensurate value.

Big data has big implications for healthcare. Perhaps more than any other future-focused activity, big data has the ability to modify the research and development that gets to the core of healthcare. Specifically, big data changes the dynamic of sampling bias. The idea that we have to select a representative sample no longer applies if we have the ability to select everyone who meets the criteria. We have a long way to go before we get to that analytic nirvana.

To the Cloud!

If you want to see me curse at a television, just show the Microsoft commercials where a tired traveler exclaims "to the cloud" so he can watch shows on his laptop. The oversimplification, and commercialization, of a technical service shouldn't really get my ire up to that degree, but it does. The cloud is not some magic entity that stores movies and television programs, nor is it the be-all and end-all for hardware-weary IT executives. The cloud is simply a service wrapped around a pile of servers somewhere. Historically these have been referred to as *server farms*, where you rent a server and you could scale quickly and easily. Not much has changed from those early days of server farms, but they were ahead of their time and lacked a catchy hook (and Microsoft's marketing budget).

I understand the appeal of the cloud. A CIO said to me recently "there is absolutely no value-add for me to continue to add hardware. I don't have the space and I couldn't possibly keep up with staffing the demand." It's true that the one thing that has changed drastically is the amount of data that the average healthcare organization has at their fingertips. The cloud does offer an easy way to provide the appropriate hardware to guarantee availability and performance.

Special considerations need to be made before you run off to the cloud. A heavy focus on the security controls of the cloud vendors is an absolute must. Not all of them are created equal and taking their word for Health Insurance Portabililty and Accountability Act (HIPAA) compliance could be very expensive. We hear of data breaches all the time, and most of these have nothing to do with the cloud. Many vendors are rushing to this because there is money in it, and in the long run it is the right thing to do for most IT organizations, whether they are in healthcare or not. Ensure that HIPAA compliance meets the letter of the requirement. Also, look at the total cost of ownership because for early adopters it may not be as good as you hope.

A hospital CIO said to me not long ago, "It sure is an interesting time to be a CIO." This comment came after a long discussion about meaningful use, tracking populations, and the lack of resources to help with the challenge. If by "interesting" he meant difficult, challenging, or crazy—I'm still not sure. But I am sure that there has never been a time in healthcare when IT or BI has been more important or more pervasive. The future is now, and much of what I *predict* here is happening on the Internet and in your organizations now. Investing in extracting, storing, translating, and preparing your data for usage will be an investment in the long term for healthcare organizations.

Notes

Kiron, D., R. Shockley, N. Kruschwitz, G. Finch, & M. Haydock (2011). "Analytics: The Widening Divide," *MIT Sloan Management Review*, Pages 1–22.

Watson, H.J. (2006). "Business Schools need to change what they teach," *Business Intelligence Journal*, Pages 4–7.

Zachry, M., & C. Thralls (2004). "An Interview with Edward R. Tufte," *Technical Communication Quarterly*, Pages 447–462.

CHAPTER 9

Putting It All Together

You may be wondering, now that we have reached the end, how and where you begin. Yes, according to the first part of the book you should start with data governance to ensure good data quality. Then move on to guaranteeing good sponsorship and leadership. Chapter 5 laid out a method for you to get to a solid technology and architecture, and all of these lead up to ensuring that you are delivering value to the end-users. Many of these chapters have templates that you can find on the companion website.

The first year of a business intelligence (BI) program is fraught with risk and challenges: lack of support, lack of adoption, questionable data quality, and so on. I hope that this book will help reduce the risk and address many of your predicaments. The likelihood that this text is a complete review of every possible issue that you will encounter is slight, but the hope is that you now have enough information to know where to aim your focus.

One of my favorite shows is *The Big Bang Theory*. Those geeks and their overzealous attempt to intellectualize everything are hilarious. In the real world, it is quite easy to overintellectualize BI. Yes, it's hard. Challenges lurk around every corner, but if all you focus on are the hard parts you get too easily distracted and forget to just move forward. After reading all of these pages I am certain that some of you feel that the challenge isn't worth the return. Even with a step-by-step guide that boils down the first year of a BI program in 10 "easy-to-do" steps, you may feel like you're at the helm of a larger project that will never reach an end point.

> *I think a simple rule of business is, if you do the things that are easier first, then you can actually make a lot of progress.*
> Mark Zuckerberg (Essany, 2012)

Strategy is important for this phase of the work. If you don't have a strategy for how you plan to move forward, every obstacle feels like the obstacle that will keep you stuck. It's easy to get distracted by trying to do it all right now. If you have a solid strategy from which to move forward, you know what to focus on today and what you will need to focus on tomorrow. To make good progress the first year, though, it's not critical to spend months or even weeks at a strategy. Identify the areas that are critically important to your organization, decide what things you will not violate as you begin this work, and move forward. This approach allows you to focus on what is important and creates good decision criteria for situations that arise. Toward the end of Year 1, we will review the concept of a strategic road map, but for now we just want to get started.

Year One

I have seen many programs get started; some begrudgingly, some with rockets, and others with carefully planned execution. How you get started, or restarted has more to do with your personal style and your organization than BI itself. It is, however, important to have some enthusiasm and passion for the work.

Believe it or not, some things can (and should) wait. You will need a data governance structure, but not a full-blown organization. You will need a data model, but there are things that need to be modeled first (the key relationships in any healthcare organization), and the rest can be added as needed.

You will need to find a leader and a sponsor, but during the first year, you really only need one strong one of each. All of this is to ensure that you deliver some value as quickly as possible. Value begets support, support begets adoption, adoption begets value, and so on. If you don't want to get overwhelmed, create a strategy to use as a guide and make sure that you follow the steps in the right order; Year 1 of your BI program will be over before you know it. Year 2 should be full of more of the same. Build out your governance, add data domains to your data model, and gain additional sponsors by continuing to focus on delivering value.

What follows is a sample timeline showing the most critical activities (or milestones) to plan for in the first year of your BI program. Durations are indicated; note that many activities will occur simultaneously.

As with most efforts a timeline for the activity is valuable. It helps everyone involved know exactly where they are and what is coming next (see Figure 9.1). It can also help you build in easy stage-gates, points at which you determine if and how you move forward. It's not enough to say that your organization will do BI; you have to prove the value and continually ask the organization for sponsorship and support.

Before I get too far oversimplifying I will break down each of these steps in enough detail for you to use this as a guide to get started.

Get Some Support

The effort associated with this step is directly related to your role in the organization. If you are an executive, your efforts to get support will take no more than an email, at least in the beginning. You will still need to find someone in your organization who can lead the effort, because you don't have the bandwidth to add this to your current duties.

Activity	Duration	Stage-Gate
Get Support	2 weeks	Did you get at least one executive sponsor and identify an interim leader?
Create Governance Structure	1 week	Have you identified at least one data steward that can act as the lead?
Projects with Value	8 days	Have you identified at least 5 projects that can bring the organization *tangible* value?
Technology and Architecture Gaps	3 weeks	Have you identified the gaps and created a plan to provide the most impact in the first year?
Cultural Preparedness	3 days	Do you know your score and methods to close the gap to improve the organizational readiness?
Kick-off	1 week	Did you expand the knowledge of the BI Program to new audiences in your organization?
Manage Inaugural Effort	Dependent on effort, but no more than 6 months	Did you have a successful deployment of the scoped effort?
Build Supporting Processes and Infrastructures	Up to 3 months in parallel with development effort	Parallel with the development effort, did you build out processes and infrastructure to support the effort long-term (i.e., Service Line Agreements [SLAs], help-desk support, etc.)?
Market the BI Program	2 weeks	Have you created a buzz in your organization around BI and what it can provide?
Train and Deploy	3 days	Have you trained all of the first round end-users on the BI tool and how to use the data to make better decisions?
Operationalize the BI Function	4 weeks	Have you reviewed all the current processes that are used to support the BI function? Did you remove any that were created as one-off's, accounting for them in a more efficient method? Do you need to add staff to ensure completion of efforts?

FIGURE 9.1 Activities in Year One

In the beginning you will need someone who is passionate about what BI can do for the organization. That person needs to be either the sponsor or the leader; it's not critical that you have passionate people in both roles, but it will help your cause if you do. Sponsorship exists at different levels so make sure that you have more than one sponsor. You can gain sponsorship over time but at this first phase it's important to have an executive sponsor who can help you with financing the effort.

As the BI leader, by now you have determined that BI is what your organization needs to move forward. In your role you see many different perspectives and needs for data, and you have seen the direct impact in full-time equivalent (FTE) that poor data processes are costing the organization. Moreover, you see the increasing impact of regulatory requirements coming and know that there is a point of diminishing returns in hiring additional people to manage poor processes.

First, you have to determine if you are going to lead the effort or recruit another individual to lead it. Some considerations to mull over:

- Do you have the time?
- Do you have the interest?
- Does your organization see you in this type of pioneering role?
- Are you willing to start it and then hand it off?

The importance of this first leader can't be underestimated. Much of the passion and enthusiasm this person will bring will determine the success of initiative in the beginning and carry it through the first set of obstacles and challenges. A sample job description demonstrates the diverse skill set required.

Probably the most important responsibility of the BI leader in the first year is creating the foundation from which BI will evolve. This requires a lot of diplomacy and politicking as you navigate your organization and attempt to get everyone on board. The right leader for BI in the beginning is the person who can put his or her head down and get to work regardless of the chatter.

Now that we have selected our leader, we have to get to work getting our sponsors on board. As we review the value chapter we know that we have to talk in terms of value to the organization, and we also know from our leadership and sponsorship chapter that we have to talk in terms of return on investment (ROI). These first conversations with sponsors will require both of these discussion points. It's worth the effort to find value that is attributable to a positive ROI within your own organization in addition to using examples from similar organizations.

Sponsorship is so critical to the ongoing success of the BI program that it is one of the first things you should secure. At this point it is sufficient to have one executive sponsor; if you have that then you can move on. As the program grows it's important that your sponsorship should grow, too, but at this stage it's not critical to have many sponsors.

Tip: Check Out Our Companion Website

We have sample slide presentations for gaining sponsorship on the companion website (www.wiley.com/go/healthcarebi).

Governance Structure

Now that we have secured the leadership and sponsorship to get started we will have to create the governance structure that will support the BI effort. Keep in mind that we are still in

Week 3 of our first year, so we have not spent much time gaining sponsorship and we won't spend much time setting up a governance structure, at least not today.

The key to your governance structure is to put together a group that will be tasked with making the work of data governance operational. These people are referred to as data stewards; a job description is included in Chapter 3. You likely have people in mind for this effort. It's time to reach out to them and determine their level of interest. In the beginning the work of stewards is similar to herding cats. Diplomacy is a vital personality trait of someone who leads the governance effort; select someone who has it in spades.

The next step is to draw out a straw man of how the governance operation will function for this first year. The governance function must ensure that the content that is released in the data warehouse is certified. The straw man should include who is doing what role and how the sponsorship roles are involved. It should also outline the definition of just enough quality (depending on what you develop, it may change) and how the governance function will determine if it is certified.

After this first effort is complete, the governance function should formalize itself. The nice thing about doing it this way is that you have some experience with attempting to govern data, so you have an understanding of what it takes to come to a successful conclusion.

Projects with Value

Now it's time to decide what you will build for the first phase. This can be harder than it sounds. As you read this you may think you know exactly what you want to build, but I would caution you to take the time to get some organizational buy-in on the first build before you jump to any conclusions. You may not think the organization really cares, but you will find out how much it cares if you move forward without asking. If this occurs you set yourself up for bad adoption from the start. It's best to take some time and ask around to validate your thoughts. If through this process you learn that the things you thought were important are actually not that important to the organization, you have to let go and build what will provide value to the most people.

Spend one week going around and asking business stakeholders what they need. Make sure you are clear that you asking everyone to be fair, but that not everything will be built in the first phase. This activity is related to the one we discussed in Chapter 4 on value. You may want to go back and refresh yourself on the types of questions that you should ask. The interviewees should represent each of the major functional areas at your organization.

On completion of the interviews, take that data and work with your sponsor to score them based on objective calculations. Then (and only then) can the sponsors rearrange based on any strategic initiatives or value drivers. You should have a nice list at the completion of this effort that could equate to the first two or three years' worth of work. This is valuable, but keep in mind that you will revisit this list often. Don't let it become stagnant because needs are changing at a rapid pace. Before you attempt to tackle your next development effort make sure you do a quick round-about of the organization again. At some point, you may want to take the time to do a more thorough survey of the data and reporting needs throughout the organization. That's a valuable activity; just don't let it get in the way of progress. It's good to have that activity run parallel to a development effort, so that at the end of one development effort you have a plan for the next one. You may not have the people resources to do that at this phase, but subsequent phases should be considered.

Technology and Architecture Gaps

Three weeks may not be sufficient for this exercise. The length of time is dependent on where your organization starts off with the technology and the architecture needed to support BI.

If this is truly your first BI effort then the gaps are significant and probably won't take much time. If you have tried before and failed, then it can be a bit trickier to navigate. It's time (if you haven't already) to ask a trusted IT colleague to assist you in the effort. A lot is riding on this activity. This is where you will determine what BI tool to purchase, and how much capital investment is required to get you where you need to be. This activity is the first and biggest stage-gate for the BI program; sometimes it may not go past this phase due to funding challenges.

Whether it's your internal resources or an external vendor, you will need to be prepared to answer the question: "How big is it?" You will need to articulate how many users you will have, what type of users they will be, how much data you will have (less important to BI vendors, but of some importance in purchasing servers), and what type of BI deployment it will be; that is, will you only use internal computers with web-enabled software or do you intend to deploy mobile devices?

If You Have Already Tried BI

Most organizations will fall into one of two categories: ones that have tried and haven't succeeded (for many reasons), and ones that haven't tried. In this section we address those organizations that have already tried. The first thing you need to assess is whether the BI tool that you used last time can get you the distance this time. It's easy to blame the tool for a bad experience, but try to be objective, because 9 times out of 10 the tool is not to blame for a bad release. Based on what the organization

223

needs, is the tool capable of getting you there? If the answer is yes continue reading; if the answer is no then skip to the next section where we discuss purchasing a new BI product.

Now that you have determined that the tool is capable of getting you there, you have to review the hardware infrastructure that the tool resides on. Based on the criteria laid out specific to number of users, volume of data, and types of usage, first assess the hardware's ability to respond within the performance parameters. Now might be a good time to do some stress testing of the system (run multiple reports at the same time to ensure that the platform can perform to expectations) to feel confident about meeting the demands. If a gap is found, then identify it and determine the investment required to close it. The recommended investment should be sure to include support for the extract, transform, and load (ETL) effort, as well as the data warehouse and BI tool.

If You Are New to BI

To do any BI work you need a BI tool to roll out to end-users. In addition, you will likely have to purchase an ETL tool as well. Knowledge about BI and ETL tools fades quickly, so it's important to do your homework. We discussed this at length and outlined the process for acquiring new products in Chapter 5.

Tip: Timing of BI Tool Purchase

Just like any other software product, BI vendors have sales goals. Vendors will be more aggressive in pricing discounts at the end of each quarter, and particularly so at the end of their financial year. There is a trade-off though—you have to be willing to make a decision and put up with a more aggressive sales cycle. The discount may be worth it.

Case Study: BI at Intermountain Healthcare: Putting It All Together

When you talk about putting it all together few organizations have done that as well as Intermountain. Its BI program was born from a physician leader in the organization whose commitment to quality changed the industry. That level of sponsorship and leadership kicked off Intermountain's commitment to data management more than four decades ago. Today, healthcare organizations looking to start in BI should look no further than Intermountain.

The current leaders at Intermountain know what created the foundation for their success. "You have to have an executive champion initiate and shepherd the building of a BI initiative. Somebody at the business or clinical level has to be the champion," said Lee Pierce, director of Intermountain's BI team.

Pierce goes on to discuss the impact that culture has on success: "Your organization has to have a culture of managing your business with data. If you don't have the culture to use and improve processes then you won't succeed." But there's no question that value to end-users is important, and Intermountain has always focused on clinical quality improvement and clinical programs that provide tangible value back to the organization.

When asked for his advice for healthcare organizations that are getting started on the BI journey, Pierce was quick to say "Don't be afraid to start, don't let perfect get in the way of good. Too many organizations focus on perfect trusted data before they get started with BI. Worrying about data being perfect in a transactional system will stall a meaningful BI initiative." He continues by advising organizations to "pick a project—something that you have organizational support for, something you know you have data for, then do something with it." Pierce recommends that organizations continue down this path selecting sets of logical data to bring into an enterprise warehouse iteratively. He advises, "Don't let the large potential scope of the project keep you from starting something. Start with financial data, it's usually good and you can get good insights. Then add clinical."

This iterative method demands that you have the means of integrating data across the sources so Pierce recommends master data management as a tool. "You should use master data management. An organization needs a single patient ID, provider ID, facility ID." His pragmatic view on architecture focuses on the business: "From an architectural design perspective, it's not one or the other, do what makes sense for the business. Build it based on requirements and make sure it provides value."

The people who do the work of BI in any organization have to be set up to succeed. "Enable as many people as possible to have access to data, particularly to those people that are creating content that they share. For your analysts, focus on giving them the right tools from the start to do their jobs." He advises that to be successful we should avoid organizational silos. "BI teams must be having conversations across the organization. We have roles at Intermountain we call data managers, and their function is to liaison between BI staff and IT. These data managers understand the business or clinical area that they represent; they know the data and they know where data is sourced from. The whole team works closely together."

Finally, Pierce discusses the user types. We have to always remember that the users in a healthcare organization are different. "Physicians will not spend a lot of time doing a lot of analysis—even if you give them a tool that will drill they won't do that. Data is important to them; they just don't want to dig. Make reports, analysis, and data as easy as possible."

Few organizations can claim the level of success in healthcare BI as Intermountain. They are the organization we all look to as a beacon as we begin our BI journey.

Considerations for Hiring a Consulting Services Firm

Perhaps this is a bit like the fox guarding the hen house, or some level of insider trading, but I have some specific ideas about how to assess consultants. Most organizations, vendors (i.e., product vendors such as Business Objects or MicroStrategy), and traditional consulting firms offer services. If you have purchased their tool and you want to use their services, that's okay, but don't always assume that they know best or have the best. Sometimes smaller service organizations are hungrier for your business and are willing to do what it takes to prove it. It's true that I am a consultant, but for much longer I hired consultants. My guidance here comes from my experience on both sides of the aisle.

- If healthcare experience is important to you, make sure they have it. Many organizations are now claiming lots of healthcare experience, but not all of them really have it. Dig deep and ask for specifics. If they don't know what a DRG (diagnosis risk grouper) is, or how ICD-10 (*International Classification of Diseases*, version 10) could impact your data warehouse, move on.

- Look for consultants who know their place. Consultants are meant to provide temporary, very specific guidance and/or assistance for a project. If you find your consultants finding new ways to plant themselves ask them to submit an application for employment, unless you like paying extra for a job an employee could do.

- Generally speaking, it's not a good idea to put all your eggs in one basket. In other words, create a preferred vendor list and let your consultants sweat it out with good old competition. It makes them a better organization and usually provides you better results.

- Channel Donald Trump. The great thing about hiring consultants is that you can fire them. If it's not working out, don't continue to invest in the consultant—it's not worth your time. Remember that good consultants will ask you if things are going well.

- Rates reflect not only the market but also the skill level of the consultant. If the cost of hiring a consultant is too high, look at all the elements that can be modified (scope, schedule, etc.).

- Hire consultants for the work that your employees can't do, whether they don't have the skills or the time. Ensure that the consultant is prepared to do a lot of knowledge transfer so your staff can learn from them while they are there.

- Good efforts for consultants to take on for you are a big influx in development efforts to meet a timeline, or very skill-specific activities such as building a data model.

Exceptions exist for each of these guidelines, but as a general rule these are good things to keep in mind if you want to hire a consulting services firm to support you in your BI initiative.

Architectural Gaps

We discussed in Chapter 5 the different levels of architecture. For this section, in the first year we are going to focus exclusively on the data warehousing architecture. We need to make sure that we have a solid foundation on which our data can grow.

You should start with the projects that you have identified that provide value. Data modeling is not an easy task and one that shouldn't be taken on as a side job because someone read a couple of blog posts. As you have read, I am a big fan of doing this work right the first time. You have a couple options for this part of the effort: The first is to work with someone on your team who has the appropriate skill set. Maybe you have this person on your team already or maybe you are looking to hire someone; either way, if you chose to go this route make sure that person understands the function and how important it is to get it right the first time. Untying the mess is not much fun and is difficult to do well. If you choose to do the work in-house, take some time to attend some training. A number of excellent books have been written on this topic, including a healthcare-specific chapter in *The Data Model Resource Book* by Len Silverston (2001).

The second option is to bring in a consulting services firm to assist with this effort. Only you can determine which one is the right one for your organization, but because it is so critical to get this first phase right I would recommend some serious consideration toward hiring a consultant. I don't take that recommendation lightly, but hiring the right consultant can mean the difference between a solid start or a massive amount of rework.

Cultural Preparedness

The question is: Is your organization ready for BI and the change it can bring? If the answer is "I don't know" then you can use the assessments provided in this book to find out. This is an important step in the first year of your program. You need to make sure that as you start, your organization is prepared to adopt the program. If not, there are steps that you can take as outlined in Chapter 7 that will help your organization get closer to being ready to adopt BI.

The next question you may have is: If my organization isn't ready do I really have to stop what I am doing? The answer to that, in my opinion, is yes. I would redirect your efforts to getting your organization ready rather than starting your BI program. You may be able to do a few key things in parallel, perhaps even purchase a BI tool, but don't wander too far into the depths of BI construction before you are certain that your organization is ready. Otherwise it's just an expensive exercise.

Marketing the Program

It's finally time to make it official! Congratulations on making it to this important milestone. The kickoff activities are really aimed at letting the broader organization know what you are starting and how it will impact them. This is tied closely with the marketing activities that we review later. The kickoff is specific to the project that the group is working on, helping those who haven't had exposure to the project learn some new things.

Even though the project takes months, the kickoff is meant to be a one-week effort at the beginning of the project. We address the kickoff activities as well as how to market the program throughout the lifetime.

Kickoff activities happen in two phases. The first should be a kickoff for the working team. On the first day have a formal

230

meeting with all team members present. Don't assume that everyone knows each other and their roles; if this is the first time you have done anything like this the odds of people really understanding everyone's role are unlikely. Take about two hours to introduce everyone, explain their roles and responsibilities and how the team should function together. Also, make sure that everyone on the team knows that it's their responsibility to market to the rest of the organization, in a positive and helpful way. As activities begin to increase people will get curious, and hallway conversations that are more gossip than fact impact the entire effort.

The next phase of the kickoff is for the broader organization. Any number of things can be done to increase the visibility of the project. I have seen posters hanging throughout the building, "lunch and learns" that explain the effort, or even an open house where people can interact with the team members and perhaps even see pictures of the BI tool (assuming it's new).

Marketing the BI program is something that most BI professionals don't really look forward to. It is, however, an important step in the work to ensure that the program has enough visibility throughout the organization. In the first few phases of development work not everyone will benefit, but if they know or hear how others are benefiting that will buy you some time. Marketing can take up a fair amount of time in a day, and with so many other activities it's important to take a step back and plan for the marketing activities that will happen over the next few months.

It's a good idea to plan for consistent communications to the user group and to the broader organization. One of the easier ways to do this is by creating a portal where you give people direct access to content, including the project plan, contact names and numbers, and any other documentation that will help users understand. Communication is the key part of any marketing effort; if you aren't out there delivering the message of what is happening (and what isn't happening) people will fill in those details for themselves.

Tip: Check Out Our Companion Website

For a downloadable marketing plan template, visit the companion website (www.wiley.com/go/healthcarebi).

Manage the Inaugural Effort

This activity will take up most of your time in the first year. It is of the utmost importance that you execute well on this first project. It's worth the time you spend on ensuring that things are happening the way you planned. There are a couple of tricks that are helpful that have nothing to do with traditional project management.

I recommend a very iterative approach to development activities for BI projects, a specific type of development life cycle. Agile methods lend themselves well to data-oriented projects. But what does that mean in practice? I would say that there are a couple of great things that the team can institute from agile methods that are good management techniques.

- Co-locate the team: If you are working through an iterative cycle then having people in close proximity is worth the effort.
- Have daily stand-up meetings: These meetings should be very brief (hence the stand-up reference) and should focus on what you are doing and what obstacles you need removed; everything else can go into a status report.
- Keep sprints short: Sprint is a reference to the time-boxed activities that agile methods use. Essentially you pick an activity and time-box it to a few weeks. You get as much done

within that time and what doesn't get done is accounted for in the next sprint.

Many of these and others are in *Agile Data Warehousing* by Ralph Hughes (2008); I highly recommend reading through it prior to getting started. However you decide to proceed is up to you, but it's important to ensure that the entire team understands how the work will be done. These details should be explained during the kickoff we discussed earlier.

Managing this effort is like managing any other project. You will have many moving parts and lots of different people and personality types working together. It won't all be blue sky and butterflies. It's imperative that the team works together well and that directive should come from the leadership of the group. Make sure that they know they can come to you at any time with a question or concern.

Each week you should pull together a status report. This status report should outline what milestones you have completed, which ones are coming, and any obstacles the team is experiencing. The report should also include an updated risk log with mitigation plans. Risk logs are a great way to keep track of the variety of issues that come up that put the project at risk. An issue or risk could be anything that jeopardizes the scope, cost, or schedule of the project. These should be documented thoroughly and, when possible, a mitigation plan (a method of reducing the risk) should accompany them. The last page should report the "burn rate" of any consultants that you are working with, plus an internal burn rate, which will help you keep track of the internal costs. A burn rate is simply the number of hours that have been worked against the amount of hours budgeted. This status report should be disseminated to the sponsors and stakeholders of the project. If you want to encourage transparency, post the status report each week to the portal.

At the end of the day, what you are managing is scope, cost, and schedule. I recommend that before you get too far into the weeds, you sit down with the sponsors and ask them what is most important to them: the scope of the work (what you will be delivering), the schedule of the work (when you are planning to deliver it), or the cost of the work (the amount budgeted). I can guarantee that at some point in the project something will come up that will jeopardize the team's ability to meet all three. When that time comes it's a good thing to have an understanding of what is most important to your sponsors. If you know that your sponsors will not agree to more money, then you'll have to tackle your issues by reducing the scope or extending the timeline. This will allow you to deal with most situations within the project team.

Build Supporting Processes and Infrastructure

As you have begun your initial development effort in your BI program you will want to start to consider the processes that will keep your BI program efficient for years to come. Creating those processes isn't a one-time activity, but in this first phase we can take some time to review processes that the organization already uses and modify some others. Many processes may need to be created to support your BI efforts.

We discussed the software development life cycle in Chapter 5, which is one that should be modified to create a repeatable process for your team to deliver content. Another major process to create is the one to support master data management. We have not discussed master data management (MDM) up to this point in the book. It is, or can be, a great asset to an organization that is taking on a BI program. I have seen many organizations spend a lot of time and money with little value provided from MDM, so exercise caution as you start this effort.

Definition: Master Data Management

Master data management (MDM) is a comprehensive method of enabling an enterprise to link all of its critical data to one file, called a *master file*, which provides a common point of reference. When properly done, MDM streamlines data sharing among personnel and departments. In addition, MDM can facilitate computing in multiple system architectures, platforms, and applications (Editorial Staff, 2006).

Healthcare has some of the most complex data around. MDM can help solve this when it's done well. Two major forces drive good MDM: the products that the organization uses to keep MDM updated, and the processes the organization modifies to (1) prevent bad data from entering the system in the first place and (2) ensure that MDM is used as the source of these data. I am not an MDM expert, but plenty are out there to provide advice. A good resource for you is a practical book on the topic *Master Data Management in Practice* by Dalton Cervo and Mark Allen (2011). This book focuses on the implementation of MDM. I would recommend reviewing the book before tackling MDM. I don't think it's critical that MDM is your first-line effort to create your BI program, but I do believe that in the long term your organization will be better off with a solid MDM strategy.

Service line agreements (SLAs) are an area where you should spend some time during the process effort. When you begin an enterprise BI effort many other departments are involved. They will rely on you to deliver valuable information and you will rely on others to provide the data. A casual agreement is fine when the effort isn't mission-critical, but once your C-level begins relying on data, it's not good enough to have a friend in a department. Therefore, it's a good idea to create SLAs between organizations that will be the most involved in the BI effort. For example, there should be an SLA between the IT team that is responsible for getting data into the warehouse (ETL) and the BI team. That is a major milestone for any BI program and without current data it will be stopped in its tracks. The SLAs should include the process for escalation when activities fail. It should also include a time frame in which errors or failures will be addressed and a minimum expectation for updates on issues. The BI team should also have an SLA on record for the business teams that rely on the data for decision making. This is a bit tougher because there are activities that the BI team has less control over that directly impact the BI's team ability to deliver data (such as lack of availability of source systems), so don't promise too much, but if you write your SLAs right you should have SLAs with those other teams as well.

SLAs are not the panacea when things go wrong. Even the best SLAs can't help when the proverbial you-know-what hits the fan. It does demonstrate the maturity of your organization to the C-level when they ask for updates, and sometimes that is all you can do.

Train and Deploy

You are very close to the end of the first development phase. If you have used agile methods, many of your power-users have likely had a fair amount of exposure to the process already. That's good because you can ask them to help you with training and spreading the word. Even though you would think that training and deployment should be more of a check-box activity than something that requires a lot of explanation, the fact is, a lot of deliberate planning is required around training your users and deploying the BI tool.

First, you will want to start planning for deployment at least two weeks before you are ready to go live. You should plan to go live on a Tuesday or Wednesday; don't pick a Monday or Friday unless you want to work the weekend. Also, avoid a major release cycle. For example, if you always release reports from the previous quarter on the fifth business day following the end of the quarter, don't release close to that date. It gives you some breathing room to let the users get used to a new system. Then decide who will get trained, how, and when. Make sure that you train users really close to a release date. For example, if you decide you are going live on a Wednesday, train the users on Tuesday. Don't underestimate how short people's memories are; even training a few days ahead can lead to confusion and delay. If you can, train the users using your own data; if it's a de-identified subset, that's better than using generic retail data. Users relate to their data much better and they won't be so distracted trying to figure out what the data means. Don't, however, mock up data for training. Mocked-up data that looks like your organization's data but doesn't reflect the reality of the data can be very confusing. The closer you can get it to reality the better off you are.

Make sure that you are prepared to deliver training in a number of different channels, such as in-person, online, or with a training manual. These redundant efforts will help solidify certain concepts better than just a quick online slide. Prepare to have extra help standing by the first few days of going live. Create the FAQs and make sure they are available, even for simpler things such as "How do I select dates?" or "How do I change my password?" Those types of questions will come up often in the beginning and it's easier to have them prepared.

As you wrap up the training and deployment week, have a little celebration that will mark the official "end" of the development effort and, by default, the start of a new one. This can be simple, but it's important that everyone understands that a lot of work and dedication went into the project, and those types of things are important to the organization.

Operationalize the BI Function

As you begin to move into your second phase you will have to focus on some housekeeping. First, you will have to formalize your data governance effort, and more information is available about that in Chapter 3. In the first phase we focused a great deal on just getting started, but we need the governance function to be a well-oiled machine by the end of the second phase. The more projects delivered into the data warehouse, the bigger the impact on the governance function. That will require many participants to know their role and how to work together.

Create a document that outlines the mission of the governance function, participants' roles and responsibilities, and how each of the separate committees work together for the same cause. You should name multiple data stewards, and their work on each of their subject areas will create documentation that will be important to most metadata as well as any master data management effort you will undertake.

Tip: Check Out Our Companion Website

For a downloadable policies and procedures template for data governance, visit the companion website (www.wiley .com/go/healthcarebi).

The next thing you may have to do is review the staffing and leadership of the BI function. If you assigned a temporary leader to get started you will want to make that selection permanent or start a search for a new leader. You also should finalize the BI team and hire any outstanding roles. I don't think BI teams need to be large to do a good job, but they need to be resourced appropriately to manage the influx of work that will undoubtedly come their way. Regulatory efforts are just the first phase of the work for BI; your organization should seek to find additional value in its data and BI is the way to do that. Don't shortchange the team resources; they need to have the time and people to be thoughtful and thorough in their jobs.

Finally, before you get too far into the second phase of development you will want to sit down with the team and your sponsors and do a postmortem of the first phase. Ask the questions that will help elicit what went well and what didn't. Spend some time assessing what went poorly and whether you have the ability to address those things. There will be instances where things went badly as a result of having rookie status, and you can't do much about that. If you find instances where the team got hung up on a decision, make sure you address the SDLC (software development life cycle) escalation procedures and decision rights. It may be a good idea to have a formal escalation path if the team can't make a decision in a reasonable amount of time.

KPIs for Healthcare

As we wrap up this final chapter on healthcare business intelligence, I think it's important to discuss the key performance indicators (KPIs) that will be part of your BI journey. Each organization will have its own version of KPIs that will be important to build onto a dashboard. Keep in mind that you can and should find some KPIs that are industry standard that will allow you to benchmark your organization against other similar organizations. For a hospital, that will be average length of stay by case mix or readmission rates. You can also look to quality indicators such as hospital-acquired infections and fall rates. For payer organizations, the list of benchmark data will have more to do with claims payment, turnaround time, and other financial indicators.

Benchmarks are important because they help you determine how you compare, but keep in mind that dashboards are designed to display a small amount of information so that the information is actionable. I advise no more than 15 metrics on a dashboard. It may seem impossible to drive your entire organization by 15 metrics, but ask yourself exactly what metrics you need to know every day to make better decisions. The metrics you identify must refresh daily to be helpful; if they don't need daily updates, they can go into a different report.

It's natural for the KPIs to go in the last section of this book because for many organizations KPIs are the last thing that they think of when they build out a BI program. Take some time to consider the KPIs and know that you will likely build multiple dashboards with different KPIs for different stakeholders. Keep in mind as you do this work that a KPI is an aggregated view of other metrics, sometimes as many as three or four, so the earlier you start defining your KPIs, the better you can prepare that data for inclusion in a dashboard.

Departing Thoughts on Healthcare BI

I am passionate about this work. Perhaps that sounds a little cliché or even naive but it's true. On the really hard days, it's that commitment that keeps me going. I firmly believe that data is the next frontier for healthcare.

Healthcare has always been deeply entrenched in data. Pasteur kept pristine records of varying data points that brought him to his revolutionary conclusion. Florence Nightingale's gift for mathematics provided her the skills to change the way that Britain looked at nursing and had a profound effect on the nursing industry all over the world. The amount of data that is required today for new drugs or adjustments to clinical care would astound Pasteur and Nightingale, yet we don't extend that level of data-focused decisions to healthcare organizations themselves.

Today, as we look at the landscape of healthcare organizations policy changes such as ACOs (Accountable Care Organization) will shape our future. Many of the new policies that came from the HITECH Act of 2009 and the Accountable Care Act (ACA) are metrics driven, from meaningful use for EHRs, to patient-centered medical home, the thing they all have in common is data. Data, more specifically, context-specific information, is our future. This future allows us to better identify our patients with particular disease-types, and perhaps more impactful, identify those patients with comorbidities that require a specific type of care. Providing more personalized care improves outcomes and reduces cost. Access to information from new websites such as patientslikeme.com creates a gold mine of information about a specific patient population and the side effects of drugs that they are on, helping drug companies and physicians alike make important decisions about pharmaceutical therapies. Information will help us better understand what works best and when, with an objective methodology not available previously, because we have access to more data than ever before.

The strategic shift from management by instinct to management by data requires a commitment to business intelligence. It is the proven method of gaining insights into your organization through data.

Notes

Essany, M. (2012). *Mark Zuckerberg: Ten Lessons in Leadership*, New Beginnings (Kankakee, IL).

Editorial Staff (2006). "Master Data Management," Searchdatamanagement. Retrieved February 2, 2012, from http://searchdatamanagement.techtarget .com/definition/master-data-management.

Juran, J. (2004). "Data: An Unfolding Quality Disaster" (as quoted in) *Information Management*, Thomas C. Redman, retrieved April 19, 2012, from http://www.information-management.com/issues/20040801/1007211-1 .html.

Data Governance Policies and Procedures

This appendix includes the template for the data governance policies and procedures. Each section has standard verbiage that can be changed. In addition, you can customize it by adding the name of your governance team wherever you see "Governance Council" and your company name wherever you see "the Client."

Tip: Check Out the Companion Website

The electronic version of this document is available for download from our companion website (www.wiley .com/go/healthcarebi).

The Value of Information Governance

Organizations today get mired down in the volume of data that they have to manage. Organizations that choose to manage their information as an asset find many market-differentiating projects that can lead to increased sales, market penetration, and profitability. Managing information as an asset requires a thorough consideration of how to manage and use data. Information governance as a function allows the business to determine how data is defined and used in a controlled and thoughtful manner. Specific benefits include:

- Improved data quality
- Consistent definitions of business terms
- Decision-making based on information (confidence in the data)
- Collaboration among business units
- Appropriate use of information
- Sharing information internally (data integration and reuse)
- Regulatory compliance
- Simplified (and known) data management business processes

Good information governance is not bureaucratic but dynamic. Although it will put parameters on data definition and usage, it will allow for modifications of its own processes if they are not responsive enough for the organization. Good information governance must be agile and highly functional to support data usage, not data control.

The keystones of a good information governance structure include appropriate participation from senior-level members of the business and a good working knowledge of business intelligence (BI) and data management concepts. The Council must also understand the value of data quality and be strong advocates throughout the organization.

Mission Statement

The Client seeks to manage information and related systems as an asset. The Client's Governance Council will serve as

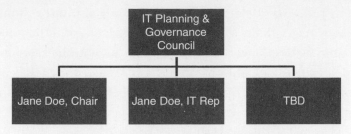

Data Governance Organizational Chart

advocates for the organization on data quality and project prioritization with the understanding that they are responsible for data and systems usage, not control. Planning and governance should not be bureaucratic but dynamic, agile, and highly functional to serve the Client's overall strategic goals—leading to increased sales, market penetration, and profitability.

The Governance Council will initially meet every three weeks. The kickoff meeting will occur in person, and subsequent meetings will be web-based. The initial agenda for the Governance Council is education, review/approval of the policies and procedures document, and prioritization. Ongoing meetings will be expanded to include project-specific updates.

Minimum Expectations for Participation

The IT representative will provide all supporting documentation to facilitate ease of decision-making. To ensure that all members of the council are prepared for the responsibilities assigned to the group, a minimum participation standard is required. Each member will be asked to assign a voting delegate, and if the first member is not able to join a meeting, a voting delegate is expected to participate. The first member should take the time to bring the delegate up to speed on any discussions or decisions that will impact his or her participation. If the council is voting, a functional area may submit its vote in absentia. If the delegate is not able to attend from each functional area, he or she can miss up to two (2) meetings a year without repercussions.

Quorum for this council is 75 percent of the voting body in attendance, and the majority rules. If your functional area is not represented at a meeting and an unacceptable decision is made, the member may appeal. IT will participate in the council meetings as a nonvoting member. In addition, other functional areas will be brought in on an as-needed basis to ensure that all aspects of an issue or topic are fully represented.

Roles and Responsibilities

Senior Staff (if separate from Governance Committee)

- Champions information governance
- Empowers governance committee
- Ensures business engagement in IT governance process including identifying data stewards and owners
- Resolves escalated information governance and prioritization issues

Governance Council

- Data owners represented by key business area, aligned with BI Governance (program)
- Creates policies and procedures associated with BI and data management
- Enforces policies and procedures
- Ensures work of data management/IT/IM team is aligned with corporate strategy
- Champions BI and data governance to broader organization

- Reviews and approves recommendations from DSWG (data steward working group) regarding terms and definitions, quality standards and thresholds

Governance Council, Chair
- Facilitates meetings
- Assigns note-taker
- Confirms and documents quorum

IT Representative
- Sends out all required documents three business days before meeting
- Schedules all meetings (including resources and additional functional area representatives)
- Keeps collaboration site updated
- Data steward working group
- Subject matter experts in their field, aligned with business units represented in steering committee
- Reviews issues with data and makes recommendations
- Ensures work is aligned with policies and procedures
- Each steward ensures proper usage, accessibility, and quality of the information within their data domain
- Establishes enterprise-wide standards for data quality and appropriate usage
- Ensures conformity, extensibility, security, and compliance

Data Steward Working Group, Chair
- Sends out all required documents three business days before meeting
- Schedules all meetings (including resources and additional functional area representatives)
- Assigns note-taker
- Confirms and documents attendance
- Keeps collaboration site updated

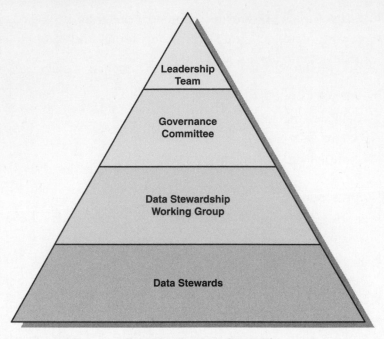

Data Governance Pyramid

Governance Committee Roster

Leadership Team Sponsor(s)
- Name, title, email, and phone
- Name, title, email, and phone

Governance Council (Data Owners)
- Name, title, email, and phone
- Name, title, email, and phone
- Name, title, email, and phone
- Name, title, email, and phone

Data Steward Working Group Representatives
- Name, title, email, and phone
- Name, title, email, and phone
- Name, title, email, and phone
- Name, title, email, and phone

High-Level Data Standards

Data quality is important to the Client. For the purpose of this process, quality of data is defined as the data falling within an expected range of values. For the Client those ranges have not been defined for each value in the data warehouse. To make progress the Client's goal for data quality will be defined in phases.

Phase 1: High-quality data will be defined as data that matches the previously reported data. The process will be as each report is built in the BI application and it will be unit-tested and user acceptance–tested to ensure that it meets the acceptable range as defined by the data previously reported.

Phase 2: As each project is built out in the BI application, the expected value range will be entered into a data quality worksheet. Those ranges will be validated in a separate procedure with the business owner of the data. Concerns over data will be addressed through the data steward process. Once the majority of data has been documented in the data quality worksheet, then an acceptance range will be defined and documented.

Phase 3: All reporting and analytic work will follow the acceptance range for each data point.

Information Governance Decision Rights

	Creates Policies and Procedures	Defines Fields, Metrics, and Calculations	Resolves Data Conflicts	Project-Based Work
Leadership Team	I	I	I/C	I/C
IT Planning and Governance Council	A	A	R	R
DSWG	R	R	A	A

R = Responsible; A = Accountable; C = Consulted; I = Informed

There can only be one group accountable for any task; there is no limit to the number that is responsible, consulted, or informed.

Glossary

Business intelligence: Integration of data from disparate source systems to optimize business usage and understanding through a user-friendly interface.

Data owner: Individual who has functional leadership responsibilities in the organization and is able to make decisions regarding definition and usage of data for their functional area (re: finance).

Data quality: Data are of high quality "if they are fit for their intended uses in operations, decision making and planning" (J. M. Juran). Alternatively, the data are deemed of high quality if they correctly represent the real-world construct to which they refer. Furthermore, apart from these definitions, as data volume increases, the question of internal consistency within data becomes paramount, regardless of fitness for use for any external purpose; for example, a person's age and birth date may conflict within different parts of a database.

Data steward: Person responsible for managing the data in a corporation in terms of integrated, consistent definitions, structures, calculations, derivations, and so on.

Information management: Information technology capability set that typically supports a data warehouse and business intelligence function.

Master data management (MDM): Comprises a set of processes and tools that consistently defines and manages the non-transactional data entities of an organization (which may include reference data). MDM has the objective of providing processes for collecting, aggregating, matching, consolidating, quality-assuring, persisting, and distributing such data throughout an organization to ensure consistency and control in the ongoing maintenance and application use of this information.

Metadata: Metadata describes other data. It provides information about a certain item's content. For example, an image may include metadata that describes how large the picture is, the color depth, the image resolution, when the image was created, and other data. There are three different types of metadata; business, technical, and application. In each case metadata represents data about the data. Business metadata is the business definition of the data. Technical metadata is the field, column, and row names of the data and application metadata is the information about data as it exists in the original transactional source system.

Unit testing: Validation method in which a programmer tests if individual units of source code are fit for use. A unit is the smallest testable part of an application. A unit may be an individual function or procedure.

User acceptance testing (UAT): Final testing phase completed by the end-users.

Business Intelligence Reporting Tool

Request for Information

This template provides a guide for a request for information (RFI) process as outlined in Chapter 5. Customize this template by adding company detail and using your own selection criteria.

Tip: Check Out the Companion Website

This template is available for download from the companion website (www.wiley.com/go/healthcarebi).

[Date]
[Company Name]
[Address 1]
[Address 2]
[City, State]
[Zip]

Confidentiality Statement

Please note that this request for information (RFI) and the information it contains is proprietary and confidential to [Company Name].

You acknowledge your request to receive this document and agree that if your firm has executed a nondisclosure agreement with [Company Name] all of the information within this document will be treated in accordance with the terms and conditions of that agreement.

As a part of the confidentiality agreement, any relationship between the bidder and any of our major competitors [list competition], must be identified in the response to the RFI. Management of the [Company Name] account must be separate from our major competitors' accounts, and any information related to [Company Name]'s account must be confidentially maintained and separate from the competitors.

Introduction and Purpose of the RFI

With this RFI we request information regarding your company and your products/services. The same information will be gathered from different companies and will be used to identify the suppliers to whom we will extend an RFP (request for proposal) or RFQ (request for qualifications) in the sourcing process.

Scope

Specific information is requested according to the form below.

Abbreviation and Terminology

[Define specific abbreviations and terminology here that relate to healthcare.]

Company Background

Provide detailed company background including acquisitions, leadership, and so on.

BI Tool Selection Process

This document will provide structure and guidance in your selection process for a business intelligence product. You can modify it to suit your needs.

Objectives

The purpose of the business intelligence tool selection is to select a [enter your reason here]. The new BI tool will support [enter your reason here].

Selection Process

[Company Name] has identified key stakeholders for each of the existing BI and data warehouse/IT teams. The working teams have defined and prioritized requirements based on existing BI application capabilities, new planned capabilities, existing functionality in the current BI tool standard, and [Company Name] technology standards.

[Company Name] is inviting a few select vendors to participate in this process based on their market leadership, industry benchmarking, and existing vendor relationships. Each company is being asked to complete this RFI and to participate in a one-day product demonstration and working session with the business and technology teams.

The [Company Name] business and technology working teams, in conjunction with the project team, will develop a recommendation and cost/benefit analysis based on the product demonstrations, RFI response, and other information provided by each vendor.

[Company Name] will select one or two vendors to participate in a pilot to prove the usability, functionality, and performance of the recommended BI tool. The vendor will partner with [Company Name] business and technology resources to quickly deliver a pilot production application with a small user base. The selection process will finish upon successful completion of the pilot and contract negotiations.

Timeline

The schedule for the BI tool selection process is:
    [modify with your activities and dates]

Activity	Completion Date
RFI release date	8/31
Review RFI with vendors	9/2
Conduct vendor demonstrations	9/12
RFI response deadline	9/15
Develop recommendation and cost-benefit analysis	9/18
Select pilot vendor	9/22

Communications

[Contact Name] will serve as the [Company Name] point of contact for requests for information, questions, and so on, related to the BI tool selection. Contract negotiation will also directly involve [Company Name]'s contract management office.

RFI Guidelines for Response

This list shows the guidelines for responding to the RFI.

- Your response should include:
  - An executive summary of your response

- An answer to each RFI requirement in the order which it appears
- References
- Pricing
- Documented assumptions
- All RFI responses must be received by [Day], [Month], [Date] at [Time] [Time Zone].
- RFI responses should be sent in electronic form [contact email].
- All questions must be submitted via email to [contact email]. Questions submitted via email will be answered via phone or email as soon as possible.
- [Company Name] reserves the right to reject any and all responses received.
- [Company Name] reserves the right to withdraw or modify this RFI.
- In the event that modifications, clarification, or additions to the RFI become necessary, your company will be notified in writing.
- Where asked to describe current processes and capabilities, please answer the questions, but feel free to suggest alternative or additional proposals. Alternative or additional proposals should be marked as such. We encourage aggressiveness and flexibility in your ideas and pricing. Explicitly state any assumptions that are made regarding your response.
- All hardware and software solutions proposed must be commercially available (i.e., GA (general availability or acceptance) versions installed in production at customer sites by [Date]).

Selection Criteria

[Include your selection criteria. Sample criteria are provided here.]

#	Selection Criteria	Requirement
Presentation Look and Feel		
1	Intuitive user interface	The BI tool is easy to learn and use for standard operational reports.
Navigation		
2	Ease of report interaction	Users can easily access shared, standard operational reports with minimal mouse clicks.
		Speed-of-thought navigation in the BI tool is important.
		The BI tool supports "mouse over text" to display metric definitions and calculations.
		A user can search for a report based on using metric names.
		The BI tool supports the display of last update dates by source system, metric, etc.
3	Report interaction functionality	A user can drill down, drill up, drill across, pivot, drag and drop, sort, etc.
4	Metadata/help functionality	Metadata is presented in a manner that is easy to understand, query, and use from a business perspective.
		The Help functionality is customizable to provide workflow help (e.g., suggestions to improve performance).
		The Help functionality is customizable to provide report descriptions and metric definitions.
		Context-sensitive help is provided by the vendor.

#	Selection Criteria	Requirement
5	Sticky/persistent parameters	The report selection criteria are automatically passed to another report.
6	Workflow	The BI tool allows a user to click on a cell and launch an external task/application. The BI tool allows a user to click on a cell and launch an external application based on a threshold. The BI tool allows a user to launch external applications.

Report Formatting

#	Selection Criteria	Requirement
7	Ease of formatting query results	Reports are easy to format and use a Microsoft Office–like toolbar.
8	Formatting functionality	A user can control report-formatting options (e.g., colors, shading, highlighting columns/rows, subtotals, total, number formatting). A user can highlight exceptions on a report. The BI tool integrates reports and graphs in a single report. Graphing features are similar to Microsoft Excel.
9	Support for report templates	Users can use predefined report templates to create new reports.

Report Printing

#	Selection Criteria	Requirement
10	Printing functionality	A user can manage report-printing options (e.g., orientation, scale). The BI tool provides out-of-the-box report viewing and printing. No custom code is required for fit-to-print capabilities.

#	Selection Criteria	Requirement

Report Distribution, Notification, and Sharing

11	Options for report access/ distribution	Users can save reports to shared folders, personal folders, and network drives. A user can access saved reports from a shared or personal directory. A user can access a list of recently selected reports. Users can self-subscribe to reports. A user can email a report to other users. A user can schedule a report to be emailed to other users. A user can select the file type for the report document or specify a link to the report. A user can select email addresses, groups, and so on, from a personal address book. A user can embed Excel macros in custom Excel report distribution (e.g., the report template contains an Excel macro).
12	Proactively notify based on thresholds/ formulas	The BI tool can send messages (e.g., email, pager) when exception criteria are met.
13	Delegation	Users can assign delegates to view their reports or personal folder.

Import and Export

14	Importing data/ selection criteria	Users can import data from external (e.g., nondata warehouse) sources and integrate the data in a report. A user can import query selection criteria (e.g., Microsoft Excel, MS Access).

#	Selection Criteria	Requirement
15	Report save functionality	Report save options are easy for a business user to understand.
		Users can save reports as Microsoft Office documents, PDF files, etc.
16	Exporting data	Users can export data to share with other applications.
		The BI tool provides an API to export data to other business applications.

Ad Hoc Report Functionality

#	Selection Criteria	Requirement
17	Ease of query setup/definition	The users can create reports on an ad hoc basis with minimal training and keystrokes/steps.
		The BI tool has a Microsoft Excel presentation style.
18	Query setup/ definition	A user can access global report objects across applications.
		Users can select from a list of business dimensions and metrics when creating reports.
		The BI tool can display different scenarios on the same report (e.g., actuals, budget) and different time periods on the same report (e.g., current week, month-to-date, year-to-date).
19	User defined groups/filters	Users can create groupings from a list of business dimensions and related attributes.
		Users can create, save, and access user-defined filters; for example, users normally run reports for certain product(s), location(s), and time period(s).

#	Selection Criteria	Requirement
20	Query preview/ execution	A user can preview a query before the query is submitted to ensure the query is valid and review the formatting/appearance. The BI tool allows a user to modify the report selection criteria and re-execute a report.
21	Query functionality	Users can set qualifiers on metrics (e.g., less than, greater than, equal to). User can create and save user-defined metrics from standard metrics. The BI tool includes built-in functions (e.g., financial, statistical). The BI tool can display metrics as a percent of total for various business dimensions. The BI tool can calculate metrics as a percent of total for various business dimensions. A report's grand total is distinct when line items are repeated in different subgroups.
22	Ranking functionality	The BI tool can calculate rank in a group. The BI tool supports complex rankings where an overall rank is calculated from other metric rankings on the same report. The BI tool supports complex rankings where the total ranking is at a different level of the hierarchy (e.g., a report lists individual store locations with their ranking within a district, and the total displays the district ranking within the company).

#	Selection Criteria	Requirement
23	Language/ currency support	The BI tool supports multiple languages (e.g., French, Spanish). The BI tool supports double byte character sets for Asian languages. The BI tool supports different currencies.
24	Excel add-in	The BI tool has a Microsoft Excel add-in to access data directly from Microsoft Excel.
25	Support for multiple queries	The BI tool integrates results from multiple queries from the same data source into a single report object. The BI tool integrates results from multiple queries from the same data source into separate objects in the same report.

Advanced Analytical Capabilities

#	Selection Criteria	Requirement
26	What-if analysis	The BI tool supports what-if analysis (e.g., create a new forecast, write data values to the database). A user can change data values on a graph and the corresponding cell values automatically change.
27	Statistical analysis	The BI tool supports statistical, trend and slope analysis.

Business Intelligence
Road Map Template

As described in Chapter 4, planning out the future of your business intelligence (BI) program is a critical step in ensuring success long term. In this appendix you find:

- Step-by-step process for creating the road map
- The road map template

Tip: Check Out the Companion Website

These templates are available for download from the companion website (www.wiley.com/go/healthcarebi).

Step-by-Step Process for Road Map Creation

1. Create the team
2. Determine interviewee
   a. Use Org Chart as a guide
3. Create Governance Council
4. Vet interviewee list with Council
5. Begin introductory emails/calls
   a. Tell them about the road map project and their role
6. Schedule meetings

7. Meet, learn, listen, and document
   a. Ask them to identify business value of their request
   b. Audio recording is ideal
8. Complete interview notes
   a. Send them to interviewees for review/approval
9. Schedule next level of interviews
   a. Repeat Steps 5 through 8
10. Collect road map team in a room for a two-day session
    a. Computer(s)
    b. Projector
    c. Whiteboard
    d. Food/drink
    e. Patience
11. Begin analyzing requirements
    a. If a lot of discussion begins on one topic, park it and move on
12. Categorize requirements
    a. Combine like statements
    b. Categorize by like solution (i.e., dashboard), you will use this in your key learning sections of the road map
13. Score requirements
    a. Schedule follow-up interviews (if needed)
    b. Use the business value score and the technical complexity score to create the final score
14. Begin estimating
    a. Estimate the top 10 to 15 based on scores
    b. Use consistent methodology for scoring
15. Create recommendation to go to BI Council

Business Intelligence Road Map

This template can be used as part of your strategic planning. The road map template can be modified to address your organization and its strategic planning process.

Assessment and Planning Template

Version x.x
Date: XX/XX/XXXX

Revision History

Date	Version	Description	Author
November, 2008		Original Template	L. Madsen
January, 2009		Edits	L. Madsen

Executive Summary

[Explain approach used to create the road map.]

The business intelligence (BI) road map is designed to shape the future of BI at [company name here]. This document explains the approach used to create the road map and recommend an 18-month plan to gain approval for the first phase of work.

[History of project.]

[High-level review of road map process of creation.]

This road map is a joint effort between [list departments]. The scope of the BI road map is to define a series of phased builds mixing foundational, tactical, and quick wins, which will significantly advance [company name] BI capability between [date] and [date].

Road Map Process

The BI road map is the result of a series of interviews conducted between [date] and [date]. The team interviewed all applicable functional areas at [company name] to gather business requirements. As a result, the interviews identified high-level business needs. The goal of these interviews was to write detailed requirements associated with each high-level business need. A subsequent set of interviews were completed with the Governance Council to identify "business case statements." Business case statements are broad concepts that are required for departments to succeed. Each detailed requirement was aligned with a business case statement and an objective methodology was used to score the relative level of effort against the business value.

The following is a summary of our key findings, level of effort, and recommendations for [company name] to achieve its future vision of leveraging enterprise information to a strategic advantage. The primary focus of this effort is [specific to each project].

The scope includes:

- Scope statement 1
- Scope statement 2
- Scope statement 3
- Scope statement 4

Key findings

- Key finding 1
- Key finding 2
- Key finding 3
- Key finding 4

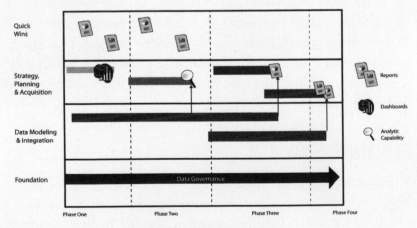

BI Road Map Timeline View

Definition

Tactical capability deliverables: Delivering requested business solutions in a tactical way, via enhanced data delivery, packaging, or presentation. Assumes we will leverage existing information assets and does not involve data facility engineering to succeed.

Definition

Strategy, planning, and acquisition: Significant, stand-alone efforts needed to capture requirements, assess needs, or acquire tooling components for future iterations. These efforts will not directly deliver business capabilities, but will provide foundational elements for future deliverables.

Definition

Information domain integration: Build out or re-architect major subject areas within the BI data facility. A set of new or modified business capabilities will be delivered as part of each effort. Deliverables will be a package of multiple requested business capabilities, revisions/enhancements to current state and creating solid foundation for additional future opportunities.

Definition

People, process, technology: Identification of organizational readiness, enterprise support, and delivery of foundational technologies.

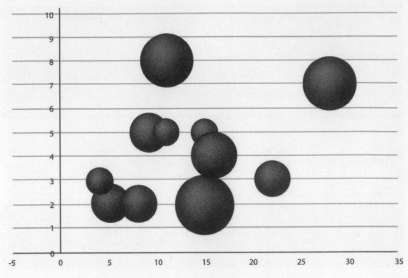

Business Value and Implementation Effort

BI Road Map Estimates Summary

The costs identified are estimated budgetary numbers to be used for planning purposes and contain uncertainty. This uncertainty is a result of the remaining variability in the solution scope. As specific scope is defined and accepted a project-planning exercise will be initiated and used to formally estimate and manage each approved solution.

BI Road Map Phases 1–3

Phase	Low	High	Average
The first phase	6,060	12,120	8,320
The second phase	4,000	8,000	6,000
The third phase	4,000	8,000	6,000
Total by Estimates Range	14,060	28,120	20,320

BI Maturity

One important key finding for the team was how important people, process, and technology are to the long-term success of our program. As we mature as a BI organization, these areas will take on a new level of focus. To ensure that we as a team continue to make progress in key growth areas we are adopting the data warehouse institute's (TDWI) maturity model. After each phase of work we will take an assessment to gauge our growth in eight areas of delivery, development, data, architecture, value, funding, sponsorship, and scope. Below is a graph demonstrating our previous score, our current score, and the benchmark score.

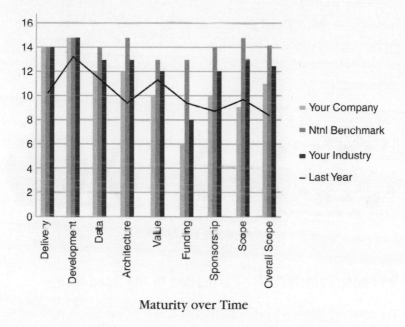

Maturity over Time

It is interesting to note the improvements in [list areas]. In some areas such as [list areas] we exceed the benchmark; in others such as [list areas] we have opportunity for improvement.

BI Road Map Process

The BI road map is the result of a series of interviews conducted between [date] and [date]. The team interviewed all applicable functional areas at [company name] to gather business requirements. As a result the interviews identified high-level business needs. The goal of these interviews was to write detailed requirements associated with each high-level business need. A subsequent set of interviews was completed with the Governance Council to identify "business case statements." Business case statements are broad concepts that are required for departments to succeed. Each detailed requirement was aligned with a business case statement, and an objective methodology was used to score the relative level of effort against the business value. The figure below demonstrates how the exercise will transition from the road map to a decomposition of business opportunities to the top-down/bottom-up business case analysis.

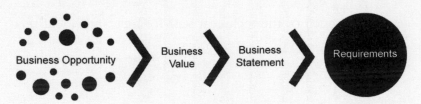

Strategy to Execution

Business Principles for Formation of the Road Map

To ensure that we knew the boundaries of decision making in the creation of the road map the business owner identified the business principles. They are:

- Primary focus is [insert detail here]
- Secondary focus is [insert detail here]

Business Needs

The following are business needs that were represented the most by the interview participants.

Primary Business Needs
- Primary need 1
- Primary need 2
- Primary need 3

Secondary Business Needs
- Secondary need 1
- Secondary need 2
- Secondary need 3

Information Domains Analyzed

Numerous information domains are included for analysis of the BI road map project. Each requirement was scored by the Governance Council or the technical staff for their individual relationship/impact.

Some of the key information domains analyzed were:

- Claims
- Eligibility
- Members
- Etc.

The full list of information domains can be found at (provide a shared file location that users can access additional information).

Key Assumptions

Below is a list of key assumptions that drove estimations and phasing in the BI road map:

- All quick wins will likely need a level of rework.
- All phases have external dependencies on business units at [company name] to define its data. Some have a need to do an application reconciliation project to determine what their source systems will be.
- For the strategy and planning exercises, the BI team will be participants, but the project should be owned by the business unit.
- We will have a pilot for each tool acquired as part of the proof of concept.
- There will be a detailed enterprise architecture road map to complement this BI road map.
- Whenever possible, solutions will include identification and utilization of existing processes and tools.
- Others.

Approach

We interviewed the business users and documented their information needs requirements and business case statements. Each statement was scored by the Governance Council for business value. The corresponding requirements were scored for the technical complexity. Then the solutions were compiled into the shared data components and type of work (tactical/ strategic, planning and acquisition, information domain integration). The results of this effort created the sequence for the BI road map.

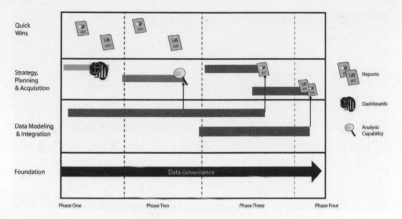

Road Map Timeline View

Participants in BI Road Map Study

[List all participants here.]

Requirements and Scoring

This section documents the findings of the BI road map assessment for each of the domains under analysis. The findings section addresses the questions that drove the BI road map and provides insight into the current state and future states of business intelligence at [company name].

Key Findings

The following is a high-level summary of key findings derived from conducting approximately [XX] interviews with representatives from each department at [company name]. The key findings are categorized under: [list categories here].

Category 1 (i.e., dashboard)
- Category key finding 1
- Category key finding 2

- Category key finding 3
- Category key finding 4

Additional Findings

To ensure that we heard all the needs from the interviews, we encouraged an open dialogue. As a result we heard requests that fall outside of the realm of this project. We excluded these items based on these criteria, for example:

- Already complete or currently being worked on
- Application or source system needs
- No business intelligence or data warehouse need

Detailed Logical Processes and Requirements

Due to the size of this information we have provided a link to this document for your convenience. The document includes all the logical processes and associated requirements with scores.
   ...\...\Link to Master Matrix.xls (nonfunctioning link)

Solutions

This section documents the recommendations of the BI road map. The following recommended solutions are categorized by phases and within phases by the following categories:

- Tactical deliverables: Delivers discreet business solutions in a tactical way, via enhanced data delivery, packaging, or presentation. Assumes [company name] will leverage existing information assets and does not involve significant data facility engineering to succeed.
- Strategy, planning, and acquisition: Significant, stand-alone efforts to define requirements assess needs or acquire tooling components for future phases.

- Information domain integration: Major efforts to build out or re-architect major subject areas within the data warehouse. A major set of new or modified business capabilities will be delivered as part of each effort.
- People, process, technology, and culture: Identification of organizational readiness, enterprise support, and delivery of foundational technologies.

BI Road Map

The purpose of the BI road map section is to provide the reader with a proposed implementation timeline of recommended projects identified throughout the process. Additionally, the road map identifies resource requirements and estimated costs.

Prioritization Quadrant

The following quadrant provides a prioritized view of the project recommendations along the measures of business benefit and ease of implementation.

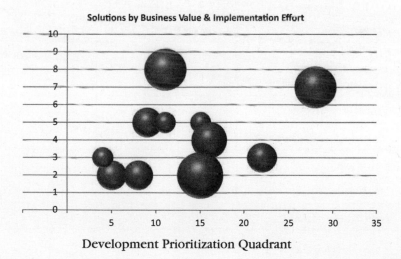

Solutions by Business Value & Implementation Effort

Development Prioritization Quadrant

Estimates Summary

The costs identified are estimated budgetary numbers to be used for planning purposes and contain uncertainty. This uncertainty is a result of the remaining variability in the solution scope. As specific score is defined and accepted, a project planning exercise will be initiated and used to formally manage each approved solution.

Global Estimating Assumptions

- Assumption 1
- Assumption 2
- Assumption 3
- Assumption 4
- Assumption 5

The following table lists the estimates for all the remaining phases of work.

BI Road Map Phases 1–3

Phase	Low ($)	High ($)	Average ($)
The first phase			
The second phase			
The third phase			
Planning and check-ins			
Software			
Hardware			
Estimates Range	$	$	$

Software and Hardware Costs

Software			
Phase	**Low ($)**	**High ($)**	**Average ($)**
Dashboard			
Reporting			
Analytics			
Estimates Range	$	$	$
Hardware			
Dashboard			
Reporting			
Analytics			
Estimates Range	$	$	$

Phase Planning

At the end of Phase 1, Phase 2, and Phase 3, the next phase will be planned. The phase-planning activities will include creating a detailed project plan for the work streams in the next iteration and enhancing the estimate for the next iteration.

Road Map Phase Planning

Phase	Low ($)	High ($)	Average ($)
Phase 1			
Phase 2			
Phase 3			
Phase Planning Range	$	$	$

The detailed estimate for these phase-planning sessions are provided below.

Detailed Estimate

Task	Percent (%)	Staff	Days	Hours	Cost ($)	Timeline (Work Weeks)	Timeline (Scheduled Months)
Task 1			83	664	66,400		
Task 2							
Task 3	5		4	33	3,320		
Task 4	15	7.0	13	105	10,458	2.5	0.6
Totals	5%	7.0	105	842	$84,655	2.9	0.7

Assumptions
- Assumption 1
- Assumption 2
- Assumption 3
- Assumption 4

Other Optional Sections
- Processes and requirements matrix
- Data warehouse reference architecture
- Road map team
- Summary of business case by phase
- Information domains delivered by phase

Business Intelligence Marketing Plan Template

In Chapter 6 marketing the business intelligence (BI) program was outlined as a key method to ensure value and help guarantee sponsorship. Marketing the program can be a time-consuming exercise so it's important that it is planned thoroughly and appropriately resourced.

This template supports the planning efforts associated with marketing your BI program. Customize it by adding your company detail and planned marketing activities. It's also a good idea to take this a step further and create a project plan to schedule the work ahead of deployments.

[Company Name Here]

[Address 1]

[Address 2]

[Telephone]

[Company Website]

Revision History

Version	Author	Date

Corporate Mission

[Insert your corporate mission here.]

Program Objective

[Insert program objective here.]

Program Audience

[Describe your audience, including any persona details.]

Communication Plan

Communication Type	Audience	Timeline

Competitive Landscape

[Describe the landscape in which you are developing your BI program. Does creating the BI program give you an advantage in the marketplace? If yes, describe.]

Marketing Objectives

What is the goal of marketing activities?

The goal of the marketing plan is to:

- [Goal 1]
- [Goal 2]
- [Goal 3]

Sample Activities

Activity	Objective	Timeline	Success Parameters
BI Book Club	Broadly share the mission and vision of your BI program to all stakeholders	Quarterly	Moderate participation
BI Luminary Awards	Broadly share the mission and vision of your BI program to all stakeholders	Annually	Minimum of 8 submissions
BI Update (brown bag)	Share status updates of the BI program build out	Monthly	5 attendees or more
BI Newsletter	Broadly share the mission and vision of your BI program to all stakeholders. Share successes of the IM program build out. Share status updates of the IM program build out.	Every other month	Link accessed at least 8 times
BI Speaker Series	Broadly share the mission and vision of your BI program to all stakeholders	Every other month	Moderate participation
BI Open House	Share successes of the BI program build out. Share status updates of the BI program build out.	Between each phase of the project	Moderate participation

BI Mission Statement

[Include your hospital or healthcare company's mission statement.]

Vision Statement

[Include your hospital or healthcare company's vision statement, if applicable.]

Status Report Template

R eporting status for any project is an important step to keep stakeholders engaged. As we outlined in Chapter 9, status for BI programs is really no different. Regardless of the management methods you use (e.g., Agile, PMI, etc.) reporting status allows you to communicate to a broader audience what is important, what needs an intervention, and what manages expectations.

To make this template more useful, update it to ensure that your project is reflected, including dates, barriers, risks, and hours used (particularly important if you are using consultants).

TIP: Check Out Our Companion Website

This template is available for download from the companion website (www.wiley.com/go/healthcarebi).

Date:
Project:
Prepared by:

Project Objective

The scope of the first phase of this work is to complete a dashboard of the key performance indicators (KPIs) that allow the management teams to more efficiently manage their operations and create a framework for a Business Intelligence Program. In addition, it will reduce the manual effort of creating the Operational Metrics used to manage the organization by completing the integration of data from disparate source systems.

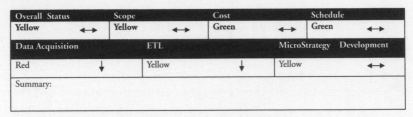

Overall Status		Scope		Cost		Schedule	
Yellow	↔	Yellow	↔	Green	↔	Green	↔
Data Acquisition		ETL			MicroStrategy	Development	
Red	↓	Yellow	↓		Yellow	↔	
Summary:							

Hours against budget

Milestone Deliverables Status over Last Period

Milestone Deliverables	Due Date	% Completed	Deliverable Status
	6/28	0%	[On Schedule]
	New 6/25	80%	[Behind Schedule]
	6/18: New 7/1	0%	[Behind Schedule]
	6/25	15%	[On Schedule]
	7/2	0%	[On Schedule]
Impact of Late Deliverables:			

Milestone Deliverables Status over Next Period

Milestone Deliverables	Due Date	% Completed	Deliverable Status	Assigned Resource
	7/1	80%	[On Schedule]	
	7/2: New 7/12	0%	[Behind Schedule]	
	6/18: New 7/23	0%	[Behind Schedule]	
	7/1	25%	[Behind Schedule]	
	7/12	0%	[Behind Schedule]	
	9/17	0%	[On Schedule]	
	7/16	0%	[On Schedule]	
	7/16	0%	[On Schedule]	
Impact of Late Deliverables:				

Risk Log

Risk ID	Description	Mitigation	Identified By	Intervention
001				I
002				P
003				N
004				E

Intervention: I = Inform Only, P = Prepare to intervene, E = Need expectation management, N = Need leadership support.

Hours against Budget

Through Date: report date the graph represents

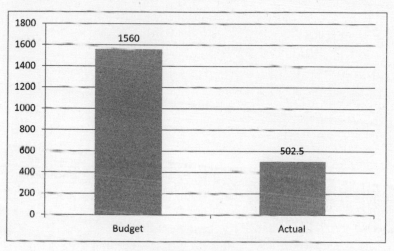

Hours against budget

Comments:

About the Website

The companion website that accompanies your purchase of this book contains a set of templates for download. These templates can serve as job aids for certain steps in your BI journey. The value of these templates is for you to not re-invent the wheel on non-value add activities but expect to modify them to meet your needs.

Each of these templates is used in my consulting practice every day. They have evolved over the years to become useful tools for my clients in creating data governance functions, strategic planning, assessing product purchases, marketing the BI program, and keeping status of BI efforts.

The link to the companion website is: www.wiley.com/go/healthcarebi

The password is: madsen

About the Author

L aura Madsen, MS, healthcare practice leader for Lancet Software, has dedicated her career to the use of data in healthcare. A passionate advocate for BI, Madsen co-founded the Twin Cities chapter of the Data Warehouse Institute (TDWI) and founded the Healthcare Business Intelligence Summit. When she's not working, Laura enjoys the Minnesota seasons with her husband and son.

Index

Silverston, Len, 229
Simplicity, 146
SLAs (service level agreements),
    28, 29, 235–236
Social media:
  for context-driven information,
    198–200
  information in EHR, 197
  as key future trend, 196
  PatientsLikeMe.com (website),
    202–204, 241
Soft return on investment, 94–96
Software purchase. *See* BI tool
    purchase
Solution architecture, 105, 112,
    131–132
"Source system agnostic," 109,
    111
Source systems, for data. *See*
    Data sources
Spolsky, Joel, 157
Sponsorship, 80–98
  in chasm of BI readiness,
    185
  communication, 26, 35, 81, 82,
    83, 89–90, 170
  definition, 68
  education about BI, 80–81, 82,
    88, 89–90
  executive sponsorship, 23, 24,
    68, 83–85, 89
  first year, 217–219, 220
  happy sponsors, 90
  as key to BI initiative, 67, 77,
    80
  leadership turnover and, 87
  leadership versus, 23–24
  levels of, 23–25, 84–87
  losing a sponsor, 87–90
  for providing value, 135
  ROI and, 25–26, 83, 90–92, 98,
    220

  in search of, 81–83, 220
  as tenet of healthcare BI, 14,
    15
  value of, 22–23
Spreadmarts, 181–182, 183, 185,
    187
Sprints, 232–233
Staff turnover, 87, 209–210
Stagegates, 118
Staging areas, for data, 6, 115
Standards:
  for data quality, 47–48, 49, 64,
    114, 249–250
  for ETL, 114
Stand-up meetings, 232
Status reports, 232, 233, 285–287
Stewart, Thomas A., 177–178
Strategic assessment, 187, 192,
    216
Strategic planning. *See* Planning
Strategy, planning, and
    acquisition, definition,
    269
Structural metadata, 21
"Suck and plunk," 18
Support for users. *See also*
    Training
  CBT (computer-based
    training), 32, 160, 237
  deployment, 237
  for executive user personas,
    154
  FAQs, 237
  first-call resolution rate, 161,
    169
  IT team, 28–29
  report consultants, 139, 140,
    141, 159, 161
  support call handling, 30, 161
  for user adoption, 26, 30,
    145–146, 147
  user groups, 75, 167, 168